Praise for E.C. Murray's *A Long Way from Paris*

"Riveting"—Scott Driscoll, University of Washington, *Better You Go Home*

"Flecked with humor and bittersweet candor."—*The Bellingham Herald*

"Oh, to be young…and a goatherd…in the south of France....Murray is both a sharp observer of the local color and a cartographer of her own internal geography, making *A Long Way from Paris* as richly textured as *fromage de chèvre*."—Langdon Cook, author of *The Mushroom Hunters,* winner of the 2014 Pacific Northwest Book Award and 2014 Washington State Book Award

"A young woman…hitchhikes from Paris to a remote farm in the south of France…her responsibilities grow, the world around her changes"—*Seattle Times*

"It is all about the simple beguiling power of internal growth. It's an adventure story, a love tale, a travelogue. Elizabeth Murray's sincere and emotionally touching account of her time in southern France stirred my soul."—Dr. Maureen Slattery, Montreal, Canada

"Captures the essence of coming of age."— *The Kitsap Sun*

'She beautifully explores her deep awareness of the land, an unfolding appreciation of hard work and the importance of family…a fascinating journey filled with wisdom, grace and compassion."—Carlene Cross, author of *The Undying West, Fleeing Fundamentalism*

Also by E.C. Murray

Life Kind of Sucks

A Long Way from Paris

E.C. Murray

Plicata Press LLC
P.O. Box 32
Gig Harbor, Washington 98335
www.plicatapress.com

Library of Congress Control Number 2014955094
Cover Design
Lindsay E. Squires and Zach LaMance

(Prepared by The Donohue Group, Inc.)
Murray, E.C. (Elizabeth Corcoran), 1954-

A long way from Paris / EC Murray.
pages : illustrations, map ; cm

Interest age level: 16 and up.
ISBN: 978-0-9903102-1-1

1. Murray, E.C.--Travel--France. 2. Authors, American--Travel--France. 3. Authors, American--21st century--Biography. 4. Farm life--France--History--20th century. 5. Goat farming--France--History--20th century. 6. Spirituality. 7. France. I. Title.
PS3613.U773 Z46 2015
813/.6

Author's Notes

My journals from 1980 and 1981 have stayed intact in their sturdy, brown paper bag book covers. *A Long Way from Paris* is faithful to those journals, as well as to the truth as I remember it which, quite honestly, may be imperfect. I changed the names of people and villages and rearranged some minor events and conversations to create a better story flow.

E.C. Murray
December 15, 2014

Map

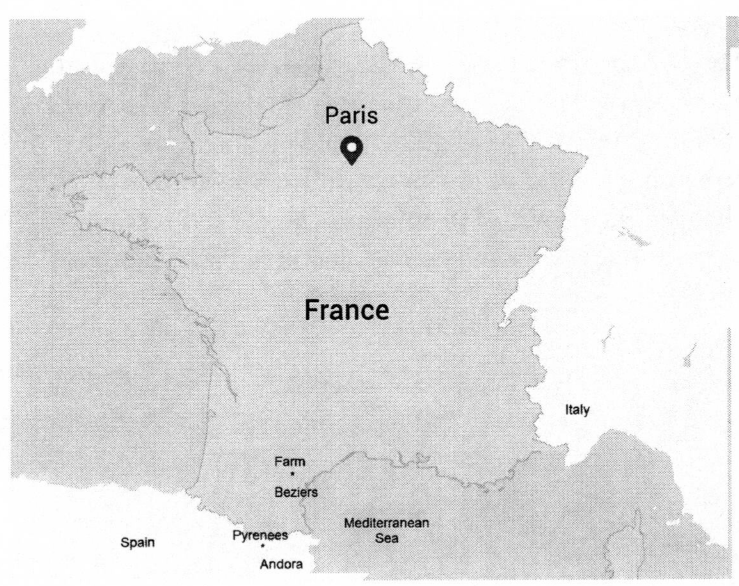

Map of France by FreeVectorMaps.com

Table of Contents

Part I. Languedoc

"The World is a book, and those who do not travel read only one page." – Saint Augustine

Part I. Languedoc

Chapter One

September 1980

We are the generation who raved at the Beatles, coveted San Francisco's "Summer of Love," and hitchhiked around the world. Born in the fifties, schooled in the sixties, we graduated after Vietnam and before AIDS. In September, 1980, thousands of us roam Europe.

I stick out my thumb, wincing at Renaults and Citroens that splash me on the exit ramp leaving Paris. Boys in tee shirts and jeans, with shaggy beards and packs at their feet, line the ramp. Line the ramp for hours. Maybe days.

I no longer count either the cars or the hours that pass under the scorching September sun, as slimy sweat pours through my yellow blouse and exhaust from cars and trucks spray me in dusty grit. I rip a chunk from my baguette, offering some to the sunburned man behind me.

When, finally, a Mercedes screeches to a stop, it stops next to me, the only woman on the ramp. I open the door and ask, "*Sud?*" as in "are you headed south?" which, of course he is, it is a southbound exit, but I am checking out the driver to see if I want to get in.

"Ah, oui. Sud," says the balding man. He stinks of men's cologne. Not a man I'd want to date, but safe enough for a ride.

"Ah, bon." I slide into the seat and roll down the window as we race out of Paris, passing suburbs of grey until the honks and hawkers of the city fade into the silence of the open pastures.

"Au revoir, Par-ee!" I say.

I'd begun my week exploring the Left Bank, dazzled by the night crowds and music and jugglers. Next, Shakespeare and Company, where I slid my fingers over soft leather books fifty years old, and imagined the conversations of Joyce and Fitzgerald and Stein. Then, to Victor Hugo's apartment, a museum now, with his desk front and center, his actual desk, where he tapped his quill in his ink jar and wrote *Les Miserables.*

And, finally, I wandered to the smoky *café* across from my exquisitely named, "Hotel California" where I ordered a *café au lait* and leaned on the tall table covered with sticky beer. I licked foam off my coffee and weighed my options. Any French I learned in school was worthless. I understood not a word. How could I possibly rent an apartment on my waitress savings? What would I eat? Really, just how does one become a writer in Paris? I had no idea.

I barely heard the taxis and tourists and screeching metros on *Saint-Germain-des-Prés* when I realized I should switch gears. Perhaps, I thought, I'll visit my long-lost cousin, the one I'd met three times in my twenty-six years, the one who lived in Languedoc, in the South of France.

Heading south from Paris, now ensconced in the cologne filled Mercedes, I rub my hand appreciatively over the leather seat, soft and comfy, and begin to daydream. What will I find at my cousin's? Will I figure out a new direction for my somewhat tattered life?

Little do I imagine the scene five short months from now:

My new French family and I shiver in their petit car. We reach the hill's crest, surrounded by snow drifts that look like pillows on all sides. Below us in the valley, a tiny, grey stone church sits alone in the snow, a parking lot on one side, a cemetery on the other. The church looks two hundred years old. Generations of men piled the stones of its walls on top of one another, by hand. A steeple peaks at the front of the small church.

We steady ourselves, skating across the icy parking lot, listening to whispers from the other people heading in. We steal into the silent, dark church, each of our steps pounding on the floor of stones, the same stones as the walls. A single ray of light shines on the pews as the door opens behind us. We proceed in the dark to the first row. I tighten my scratchy blue scarf around my neck, clasp my frozen hands together, and watch my breath rise in white wisps.

The priest, robed in black, directly in front of us, begins to speak in foreign words with a voice that honks, nasally, grotesque. I peer over my shoulder, noting the seats are scarcely filled. Almost choking on the dense incense, I chew my lips, not understanding a word, not knowing if it's French or Latin. Though seated with the family, I feel alone.

When the priest finishes, a cough sounds from the back of the church. We follow the priest down the center of the dark aisle, scuffing the stone floor, inching through the viscous air laden with smoke and desolation, as tangible as the cold of our fingers and the icy drips which fall from our noses.

Men lift the casket and carry it outdoors. Following alone and in pairs, we leave the dark church and blink at the bright, grey daylight, a sharp contrast to our eyes. We mill through the snow behind the church until we reach the spot where the casket lies in front of a simple white cross. We no longer muffle our tears. Sobs, loud and fierce, sound even more poignant against hardened icy snow. The casket can't be buried. The ground is frozen. Instead, we stare at the brown wooden box while the priest utters a few more words.

The gold chain on the driver of the Mercedes sparkles in the afternoon light. My daydreams fade and soon I drift to sleep. A minute later, or an hour later, who knows, I jolt in my seat and my eyes spring open as the driver's hand slithers up my leg, under my skirt. "What are you doing?" I shout, slapping his hand. "Stop it!" I sit up to see that we've exited from the freeway and are driving down a back road, parallel to the main highway. "Stop!" I gape out at the acres of barren fields. "Stop!" I scream again. The driver's eyebrows furrow, perplexed. He swerves off the road and smashes into a post, which gives me a moment to grab my backpack and leap from the car. He backs up, and roars into the French countryside, flinging a trail of dirt behind him.

Sobs erupt from my shaking body. I am so lucky to have escaped unharmed. Thank God. Still, my tears won't stop. I'd been fat for ten years, but now I've slimmed down. When I lost sixty pounds a year earlier, the weight left my body, but not my mind. I still see myself as a fat person. Is it easier to become slender in the body than slender in the mind? Hitchhiking used to seem safer when I weighed one hundred ninety pounds. Or, at least, that is my illusion. Hitchhiking is, indubitably, a dangerous enterprise. Especially for me, an American woman, stuck in the middle of who knows where, between Paris and Montpellier.

I wipe my eyes on the tails of my blouse and catch my breath, trying to get my bearings. A field of red poppies separates me from the deafening highway, the highway where I would have been, had I not fallen asleep, had my driver not pulled off the road to do who knows what.

There is only one option. Forward. I step over strips of cassette tape, mangled in the field like spaghetti, and make my way through the poppies to the freeway. I say something along the lines of, "Oh, fuck!" and stick out my thumb until the sun fades, casting shadows across the highway.

A car stops, a Peugeot, and I hop in. The man, thirty-ish, has black greasy hair and a pointy nose. He smokes a hand-rolled cigarette and flicks the ashes out the window. I hope for a long ride and my breathing finally slows and my heart notches down a beat. The moon rises and the sun vanishes, and I begin to relax.

Suddenly, out of nowhere, the driver pounds on his brakes. I fly forward, hitting the dashboard and scream. He reaches across me and opens my door. "Get out?" I ask.

"You want me to get out? Here?" The road is deserted, empty, no car, person, house, only a strip of asphalt before us and behind us, dark under a thick canopy of trees. "*Ici?* You're dropping me off here, in the middle of nowhere?" I try to say in French.

He is. I'm not sure which scares me more—the driver or the forest. I yank my pack from the backseat. What happened? Did he realize I have no intention of having sex with him? I step out of the car and he slams my door, speeding away, his red lights dwindling down to dots before they disappear entirely. I remain under the gloomy trees feeling like I'm in a Hitchcock movie.

The road is black. I mean pitch black. The darkest I've ever seen. The forest primeval. And silent. Not a single car, no human, no animal. I begin to walk, listening to my footsteps clap against the road. The trees smell green, alive. Oh, I hear something. No, that's just my heart. Thump. Thump. Thump.

Heading down the road, I whip my head from side to side, ready for whatever leaps from the trees - an ax murderer, a UFO, a wild boar. I sing, my voice quivering. I stop to listen. A breeze rustles some leaves. How can a road be so dark, a forest so dense?

Most places, I'd see stars or the moon, but here, under these impenetrable trees, I see nothing. I try to listen to my breathing. I squint and spot something, far in the distance. A light. I pick up my pace, still jetting my eyes from side to side. I run down the middle of the road, faster and faster toward the light. It's a motel. A motel light! I'll have a place to sleep! As I get closer, I think Bates, as in Bates Motel.

Psycho. The building sits all alone in the middle of the forest, rectangular and concrete. The only light flashes, "Motel." Or rather, "Mo_ el." I bang on the door. *"Bonjour? Bonjour?"* Part of me wants someone to answer, and part of me imagines Norman. No one answers.

Almost relieved, I wander around the corner and lean my pack against the building, unroll my sleeping bag, and climb in fully clothed. I dig through my belongings, and retrieve my cassette tape recorder. I drop in a Grateful Dead tape, and when Jerry Garcia starts singing *Sugar Magnolia*, my jaw unclenches, my breath slows. Though still afraid, the pines surrounding me smell like Christmas and comfort me. Perched up against the wall to stay alert, as though I am on watch duty, I let my mind roam. Where is Garner? How are my parents? Can one really die an agonizing death from fright?

I make it through the night. Perhaps I even sleep. A stream of sunlight peeks through the trees in the morning, and I brush needles off my sleeping bag, roll it up, and stick out my thumb once again.

One more night and four rides later, a truck grinds its gears to a halt and drops me off in the little village, my destination.

"Merci, au revoir." I say to the last driver. I jump down from the tall truck, watch him disappear around a curve, and from my pocket I pull out the wrinkled map my cousin drew me a few years ago. I am near his village, and spot a hill, a path, and miraculously, I hear Elton's voice as he rambles from his stone cottage, deep in the woods.

"Elizabeth," he says, surprised.

“Elton!”

We hug, lock arms, and stroll to his tiny home which has no electricity or running water and just a small fireplace for heat. “It’s wonderful to be here. I’ve been hitchhiking for three days.”

“Well, it’s great to see you.” Elton says. We hardly know each other, third cousins and all. I’m sure when I saw him in San Francisco two years ago, and he drew me the little map, he never expected I’d ever visit. “Sure, come see me in the South of France.” Ha. Ha. But I am here and he is gracious. We pick vegetables from his garden, which overlooks forests and mountains, no sign of civilization in sight. We laugh and laugh some more. I am so relieved to be off the road.

In the evening we hunker down in front of his fire, drinking chamomile tea. Saffron flames cast a glow on the stone walls. I sigh. Safe at last.

“What are you doing here?” Elton finally asked. "What are you doing in Languedoc?"

"Languedoc. That name wasn't on my map."

"Languedoc-Roussillon is the name of the region now. In ancient times, Languedoc was the province in southern France, that extended along the Mediterranean Sea, from the Rhone Valley to the north eastern border of Spain.”

“Were there Crusades here?” I ask, trying to remember my history.

“The Albigensian Crusade, Christian against Christian." He pours more tea and blows on the embers. "So, really, what are you doing here?”

I tell him about graduating from college and falling in love with the wrong guy, Garner, who headed to the oil fields of Utah. "When Garner and I went our separate ways, I remembered my dream of being a writer in Paris. But, that didn't work out, so I came here."

Elton and I weed his garden for two days. Beads of sweat from the stifling September sun snake down my neck. "I'm not sure what I want to do," I say. "I always wanted to be a writer, but somehow that never happened."

I throw a handful of weeds into the pile. "I kept journals for ten years and I wrote poetry, but that's about it." I lower my voice. "Actually, for whatever reason, and there are a few, I never really believed in myself." The sun burns and I feel my pores open in the steaming heat.

"Have you ever heard of the Saturn Return?" Elton asks.

"No."

"Well, in Hindu astrology when the planet Saturn returns to the same point in the sky that it occupied when a person was born, that person crosses a major threshold and enters the next stage of life. With the first Saturn return, a person leaves youth behind and enters adulthood. Some people believe that age twenty-six is the age of a person's Saturn return."

I scratch my nose, swab a drop of perspiration from my cheek. "So, you think I'm entering a new stage in life?"

Elton doesn't answer.

"By the way, when that guy was trying to molest you, what did he say when you screamed, 'Stop! Stop!'"

"Nothing." I pause. "Why?"

"Because 'stop' in French means 'hitchhike.' While you were pushing him away, he was hearing you yell, "Hitchhike! Hitchhike!"

I try to keep from smiling, but I can't.

"So, Elizabeth, would you like a job?"

"A job?" I clear my throat. My waitress savings will last longer if I have a job. I can stay in Europe a few more months. Maybe a year. It might be an adventure. "What kind of job?"

"I have a friend who needs a goatherd."

I toss another fistful of weeds into the pile and laugh, thinking he's joking. He isn't. "Are there really goatherds anymore?"

He nods.

"Really?" I ask. "Goatherds? Like in *Heidi* or *The Sound of Music?*"

"My friend, Camilla, needs someone to milk her goats, lead them up the mountain, and keep them safe. Would you like the work?"

"Goatherd?" I grew up in Holyoke, Massachusetts. In my neighborhood, dads were doctors and lawyers, owned jewelry stores and shoe stores, ran newspapers and paper mills. There was prep school and college, which branded you for life. "There's no way in hell I can be a goatherd."

"Sure, you can. You can do it. You might have a steep learning curve." Elton's mouth betrays a glimmer of a smile. "I think you'd like it. You'd make cheese, help the family with chores. Primarily, you'd herd the goats, though."

I suck in my lips. "I'm a city girl. I barely know a sheep from a goat."

"Yeah, but you'll learn."

I rub my forehead and think. The truth is, I want something vague, amorphous. I feel something tugging on me, in me. Maybe, just maybe, if I herd goats in the mountains of southern France, I'll figure things out. Certainly, I'll never have an opportunity like this again. Plus, I'd have more time to get over that man I left behind.

I smell the soil from Elton's garden, fresh, rich, alive. The sky overhead is as blue as a fresh water lake. I think of people who pay Outward Bound to survive outdoors, who learn to become strong and confident. This would be sort of like that. Except, I'd get paid. I am neither strong nor confident. Could I do it? Who knows? Maybe I'd get rid of the self-doubt that's plagued me for years.

"Okay," I finally say; "I'll be a goatherd."

Elton walks to town to phone Camilla Fontaine to tell her that she has a new goat herd, and the following week he flies back to San Francisco for the winter.

The market in the village square buzzes with women, for it's mostly women, shouting, flailing their hands, beckoning. *"Beau tissu à vendre!"* calls one, her hands wrinkled, her nails stubbles. *"Fromage de chevre!"*

"Pommes de terre!" calls another, her apron not quite covering her rolling belly.

I pass the line of vendors with their rickety tables and reach a broad ancient oak tree. Relief from the brutal heat. I slump against the scratchy bark, drop my pack at my feet, relish the shade of the leafy boughs. Stucco buildings surround the town square, their shutters faded blue, their roofs red clay. The air fills with garlic and goat cheese and dust.

"*Ay liz a bet a!*" A woman, a few inches shorter than I, bounces toward me, stretching out her arms. "*Ay liz a bet a!*" Her onyx eyes shine behind her old-fashioned, tortoise-shell glasses. She kisses both my cheeks. I suppose she recognizes me because I'm the only person with a backpack, the only American, the only twenty-six-year-old in a tee shirt and jeans in this six block village in the South of France.

"Camilla? Camilla Fontaine?"

"*Ah, oui!*" She scoots her glasses up her nose and tosses my backpack in her flimsy vehicle, part car, part truck, but tiny, like a Volkswagen bug. I slam my door that's as thin as a cookie sheet, and Camilla begins to chatter, twirling her wrists in acrobatic motion. Neither she nor her family knows English. I took French from fourth through eleventh grades, so you'd think I'd understand, but, no. A word here and there, but mostly it's lost on me. I clutch my seat as Camilla veers around corkscrew curves up the mountain, past fragrant sage and vineyards and rock walls crumbling into scattered stones.

I bet you'd never believe—I imagine myself speaking with Garner—that I made it all the way to France. How do you like working on those stupid oil drills? I'm so glad I didn't go to Utah with you. Perhaps I'm a city girl, but I'm going to work on a farm herding goats, and you can just drink yourself to death as far as I'm concerned. Of course, I don't really feel that way. The truth is that I'd like to show that love of mine these majestic mountains and introduce him to Camilla. Where is he, that wiry, black-tee-shirt-man who churned my heart?

I cock my elbow out the car window. A breeze brushes my face, and overhead, a lone bird drifts, flaps its wings, flying beyond the horizon. Forty minutes later, Camilla slows the car and drives onto flattened dirt—no semblance of a driveway. A rooster squawks, hopping around the car. He jumps onto a pile of scrap concrete heaped where I'd expect to see a lawn.

I stare at the two-story house. The stones from which it was built look like they were piled by hand, perhaps a century ago. The solid walls with only two windows, the size of eight by five inch books, are as fortified as an ancient prison. Another stone house is squashed next store, while across the road, two other ancient homes nestle together. Beyond them, only hills leading to mountains, and rocky fields leading to forests. I inhale the scent of cool mountain air, dazzled by this endless vista of nature.

Ay liz a bet a!

I hustle behind Camilla to the back, to the home's only door, a thick, hand-hewn slab. We're greeted by thyme-scented soup on the wood stove, which occupies the back corner of the kitchen. I freeze a moment, dazed. Grey cement walls meet the grey cement floor, like an unfinished basement. A laminated table covered with plastic washing bins sits in the center, while underneath I spot a stack of buckets. Pans hang on hooks from above, next to the one bare light bulb which dangles from the stone ceiling. What am I doing here, I wonder. I've embarked on an adventure sight unseen, and now it's like I've traveled back in time.

"Viens, Ay liz a bet a!" I understand a little French, and the urgency in Camilla's voice cannot be mistaken. Clearly, there is no time to waste. I throw my pack over my shoulder, and follow Camilla up the ladder that leans against the kitchen wall. We reach a loft with a mattress where Camilla and her husband sleep, and beyond a curtain, a separate space for the mattresses of their sons. Next, we climb a second ladder, to a closet-sized space, with eaves so low I bump my head.

"This is where you'll stay with my daughter, Marie." I think that's what she says. This is my room? Half a mattress on the floor with no bed in a loft so low I cannot stand?

Camilla descends and I stuff all my possessions (aka my backpack) under the eaves. Perched on the mattress, I wrap my arms around my knees, and shake my head, astonished by this ancient world. In the kitchen below strangers speak incomprehensible French. I remember my bedroom growing up, pale blue with white lace curtains just above our kitchen. I'd hear Julie, our housekeeper, opening cupboards, humming, baking my favorite, lemon meringue pie.

Julie and my Mom kept our house immaculate. I never cleaned a floor or cupboard, washed a window or car, scrubbed a bathtub or refrigerator. I didn't do dishes. Although we drove Fords and Chevys, and our house wasn't grand, my attorney dad liked luxury. If you want to camp, you send your kids to the Berkshires. If you stay at a hotel, it's the Hilton. If you barbecue, it's in a bow tie with a gin and tonic in one hand and an oven mitt in the other.

Prep school, Lilly Pulitzer dresses, elocution lessons—that was my childhood.

I was seven before I realized our faucets weren't monogrammed, that the "H" and "C" weren't for my Dad, "*Hugh*" "*Corcoran*" at all. Everything else might be monogrammed, but not our faucets. At least I needn't worry about that here in France, because there is no faucet. No toilet. Or running water. Or heat.

I crawl down the two ladders, feeling—well, not afraid, not after my terror hitchhiking from Paris—but my heart is beating quickly, and I sure wish I could understand more than a couple of words. Still, I love adventure, and I love exploring, and this is one hell of an adventure.

Camilla wears a blue paisley shoulder-to-hip apron which I'll come to recognize as her daily uniform. *"Ay-liz-a bet-a,"* she calls, handing me a knife. She peels a section of a potato and tosses it to me. Whew! Something familiar. I can peel, certainly. I look more closely. Thirty potatoes. The knife is dull. I curl my hair around my ear.

Camilla dives into her work with the zeal of a Parisian chef, throwing logs on the fire in the cook stove, washing pots and pans, and then she returns to me. "*Vite! Vite!*" She swipes the knife and peels the potato in seconds. I quicken my pace and eventually finish the stack. "Now, slice," she apparently says. Once again, she models for me. Thunk! Thunk! Her knife slams through the potato pounding the table. Her potato is sliced. For me: zip, zip, zip, and about eight more zips. I cut the second one, peeking up to see Camilla scowl.

With its two-foot-thick stone walls, the house looks huge from the outside, but once inside there are only two rooms downstairs, the kitchen and the *salle à manger*, with an attached *fromagerie*, the cheese-drying room. Camilla hands me a basket of bread to carry to the *salle à manger* which may translate to "dining room," but which is, in fact, the Fontaine's a place for eating, entertaining, studying, playing, and skinning an unfortunate, dead goat. A huge handmade table fills the room from one end to other, with hard wood benches on both sides where we gather for dinner.

"Ah, bonjour!" Two of Camilla's children, Marie and Louis, ages fourteen and eleven, rush in, pop two kisses on each of my cheeks.

"Ah, bonjour," I say.

With skin white and delicate like fine China, Marie's face is framed by dark, shiny hair that reaches below her shoulders. Her sexy kitten smile radiates like a girl much older than fourteen. But, as we drink our potato-leek soup, she elbows her younger brother and whines like an eight-year-old until Camilla shakes her spoon. *"Arête!"* she yells. "Stop it!" Louis, small like his Dad, bounces on the bench like a spring, apparently telling a long story about something in school, waving his hands as the French always do.

Across the table, a black cauldron hangs on an iron hook over fiery logs in a fireplace that spreads across one entire wall with a stone hearth nearly as large. The other three walls are bare grey cement, with one bureau snug in a corner. Camilla's husband, Jacques, with a rugged face and translucent blue eyes, grunts at me. He suddenly lunges across the table, grabbing bread from the basket like an eagle snatching a rodent from a field. He plops back down and chews nonchalantly, his mouth open with every bite.

My mouth falls open. I'm used to, "Don't eat until the hostess sits, fork on the left, spoon on the right, take small bites, napkin in the lap, chew with your mouth closed, never talk with your mouth full, and elbows off the table." I tap my foot nervously on the cement floor and watch the family eat and drink in silence like nothing odd happened at all. A little giggle creeps slowly up my throat. I try to suppress it, but my laughter, which has always burst out at the wrong time, builds and builds and finally it explodes like a bursting bottle of champagne, a rip-roaring belly laugh. Tears roll down my face. I bite the side of my cheek to stop my laughter, but I can't muffle myself. The family stares.

"Why is she laughing, Mama?" Louis asks, his green eyes wide, perplexed.

"I don't know," says Camilla. The whole family holds their forks mid-air, like a TV show on pause, and stare at me. A moment passes, and they continue eating.

Oops.

Oh, Garner, Garner, Garner. How I'd love to show you this. I've gone back to the Flintstones era.

After our evening supper, Camilla gestures me outside in the dark to a vehicle that looks like a miniature oil truck. It supplies our water. Camilla takes the attached hose, fills two buckets, and carts them into the *salle à manger* where she pours the water into the cauldron to boil for dishwashing.

I fill two pails and tug on the metal handles. They don't budge. I try again. The handles slice my palms, water sloshes over my shoes, and I feel like I'm heaving boulders. I wiggle my wet toes, inhaling the cleanest air I've ever breathed. The outline of the mountains shines like black satin in the moonlight under the star-filled sky. Goats' bells tinkle from the nearby barn, and the scent of sage lingers on the breeze. Other than the house and the barn, there is no sign of civilization. I'm enchanted—this sense of wholeness, this splendor in nature, this connection to the earth and sky and air.

"Ay liz a bet a!" Camilla shouts. *"Dépêche!"*

Ok, got it!

Again, I yank on the bucket handles helplessly. Finally, I drag one pail with two hands, waddle to the table inside, spill water everywhere, and go back for the second. I glance at my drenched sneakers, and at Camilla's frown. Shit. Between peeling potatoes and carrying water, I get an "F" for my first day on the farm.

Later that evening I lie awake, my face inches below the eaves. Marie rolls over next to me, grunts, and breathes quietly again. Someone tip-toes up the lower ladder, past Camilla, and flops down on the other side of the curtain. I can hear every snore, every mash of a pillow, and if there were sex, I'd hear that too.

I'm bummed. I can't carry the stupid buckets. Or understand much French. Or work fast enough for Camilla. Still, there's something in this air, these mountains, this simple lifestyle that calls to me. For whatever reason, this world back in time feels right.

The next morning, I'm alone. Marie's already at school. Pulling the sheets up to my chin, I savor a few moments under the covers, smell the acidic coffee scent that wafts up from the kitchen and take a breath, let it go. Okay. Time to be a goatherd.

Camilla, again in her blue paisley apron, scrubs plastic cylinders, and smiles. "*Bonjour, Ay liz a beta!*"

"Goat stew" she says, nodding to the pot. "For today's noon dinner."

At least, I think that's what she says as she feverishly scrapes the little holes that dot the sides of the six-inch cylinders. When she speaks slowly, using the French vocabulary I learned in school, I can sometimes understand. "Did you sleep well?" she asks. When people talk jet-plane fast, like at last night's supper, I miss it all. This morning, Camilla's voice lilts, cheery and friendly, but I don't catch any more of her words.

I carry my small cup of chicory into the empty *salle à manger*, where the cavernous fireplace and bare stone walls remind me of Plimoth Plantation, the replica of the Pilgrims' village in Plymouth, Massachusetts. A basket of bread, a box of milk, and an empty bowl wait for me on the table. What do I do with these? I'm stumped on how to eat breakfast. I scrutinize the milk box that's the size of a small box of Quaker oats. Unrefrigerated milk? Every moment is a new adventure, a new puzzle.

After several minutes, I pour the milk in the bowl. Like having a bowl of cereal without the cereal. I add a dash of my chicory coffee and spoon down the milk in the bowl, rip off a piece of the *baguette* and dunk it like an Oreo. I hope I've eaten my breakfast right. Not an auspicious start.

A tan, blond man strides in. Mmm. Sexy. Michel, the Fontaine's seventeen-year-old son, with puffy lips and flirtatious eyes, must be the one who came in late last night. According to my cousin Elton, Michel hitchhiked to Tunisia in northern Africa at age fourteen. His eyes gleam a soft green. Though I am nine years older than he, I know I blush.

Michel says something with a mischievous smile, like he's making a joke. I nod like I understand, but I understand nothing. He curls both hands and moves them up and down. Time to milk the goats, I suppose. I follow him out the kitchen door, down a short hill to an unpainted barn from which I hear moos and baas and gentle bleats. He opens the squeaking, heavy door of the barn, and when the dark lightens, I see my tribe: forty-two goats, twelve sheep, and an enormous orange cow. Wait a minute. I'm not just a goatherd? I'm a goatherd, a cowherd, and a shepherd, too? I am so screwed.

The only barns I've seen were at the "Eastern States Exposition," the New England version of a county fair. There, roofs towering thirty feet high rose over clean barns with immaculate stalls decorated with baskets of fresh hay and flowers and sometimes ribbons displaying wins from 4-H competitions. I wrinkle my nose. Manure? The animals shuffle in their stalls, which actually aren't stalls at all, but loose partitions divided with handmade gates of rope tied to slender branches.

I swallow, shake my head, and prepare myself for what's coming next. Milking. Oh, I hope I can do this. Michel unties a rope partition, freeing several goats. One strolls toward us and stops, carefree like a shopper browsing in a store window. Michel grabs a dirty silver bucket, turns it upside down to sit, and gestures for me to stand and hold the goat's horns.

Hold those prongs growing out of this animal's head? Eeeww. I hesitate, but take the horns like I'm steering a car, and though the creature shakes his head half-heartedly, he settles down, and I relax a bit. Michel places the clean bucket he brought from the kitchen under the massive goat's belly. "*Ici*." He rubs the tiny teats, and I feel the milk's warmth as it splashes into the pail.

My turn. I sit on the bucket, the rim digging into my buns, and begin. You've got to be kidding. The soft, rubbery teats are small—only a few inches long. "Like this." Michel demonstrates that I should hold the front with my first three fingers, and rub down with my thumb. I twist my fingers this way and that, like stretching taffy. The other goats shuffle and snort, waiting their turn. I rub my thumbs up and down, pull, push, but not a drop.

Feeling useless, I rise from my bucket and Michel takes over, milking a mahogany-colored goat. I fail to milk goat number two, and goat number three, and resign myself to holding the goats' heads as Michel milks the rest of the herd.

I trail Michel back to the house, my head down. Damn. So much for my new job. I can't even milk a goat. At noon dinner, Camilla, Michel, Jacques, and I assemble on the wood benches to eat goat stew that's a bit sweet with the light flavor of Languedoc wine. Delicious. Or should I say, "*Délicieux?*"

"*Bonjour*." A tall man and woman stride into the *salle à manger*.

"*Bonjour, Madam*," they say to me.

"*Mademoiselle,*" Camilla corrects them. An unmarried woman is always "*Mademoiselle.*" And to me she says in French, "These are our good friends from the nearby village, Marian and Jean."

They tip their heads, staring at me, an oddity. "*Mademoiselle. C'est vrai?*" A single woman? American? In the depths of the mountains of Languedoc? I shift my feet, uneasy. Perhaps they've never seen a single woman, twenty-six years old, who is neither ugly nor scarred nor deeply flawed. I feel their unasked questions. Why aren't you married? Where are your children? What are you doing in this wilderness?

If asked, I'd say that growing up in Massachusetts, I dreamed of travel. Yearned for it. I spent my first sixteen years in the same house that my Mother lived all her life. By eighteen years old, I'd barely left New England. Initially, I traveled "way out west" to Ohio Wesleyan for college, and a few years later, I ventured farther, to Eugene, Oregon.

Eugene attracted men and women from all over the country searching for alternatives: alternative food, alternative medicine, alternative housing. Single and free and independent, many of us attended the University of Oregon and smoked pot and ate acid and reflected on the meaning of the universe, which was perfect for me, a philosophy major.

In most parts of the country, men and women age twenty-six had completed their education, married, had a child or two, a mortgage, a car payment, television, and credit card debt. Not me. I read Jack Kerouac voraciously, feeling like "The Woman on the Road." My possessions were few. I shared attics and garages and houses marked for demolition; rode my bicycle or took a bus or stuck out my thumb; volunteered at the crisis clinic, read piles of books, and rarely watched TV. I hitchhiked up to northern British Columbia, down to LA, and east to visit in Ohio and Massachusetts. During that time, only one friend married—in a teepee with a hash pipe—but I was in St. Louis that summer.

It wasn't all easy. At one point I broke down and spent a year getting back on my feet. But I loved the open road, and wearing size twenty pants, I had the illusion of safety. By the time I arrived in France, I'd lost my extra weight, had visited forty-eight of the fifty states, and had graduated from college after seven years. Still, no husband, child, mortgage, car, TV, or credit card. I was indeed, "*Mademoiselle.*"

In the Fontaine's *salle à manger,* Jean kisses me on the cheeks, and Marian quickly follows suit. With his olive sweater hanging loosely over his torn pants, Jean's face appears tinted green, it's so pale. He drinks wine with Jacques, while Camilla, Marian, and I head to the kitchen and peel apples for dessert.

Marian fascinates me. She pulls back her hair that falls in waves to her shoulders, revealing a solemn face. Her raw, worn, and dirty hands don't match her gracefulness; her tall, thin body that moves with poise and beauty, like a model on a runway.

With one flick of the wrist, Marian peels apple after apple, twirling her knife quickly around each fruit, creating just one, long, spirally peel for each apple. How did she do that? Just one peel for the entire apple? So fast? For every apple I peel, she flicks through five. She smiles at me and speaks, but it could be Russian or Swahili because I cannot understand a single word. Her tone warms me, though, and I imagine us becoming close friends when my French improves.

When Camilla speaks slowly and gestures, I catch a word or two. But not with Marian. When Camilla and Marian chat, Camilla's shoulders drop and she laughs lightly, as though she has no cares in the world. They speak rapidly to one another like the best of friends.

After cake, wine, and conversation, inscrutable to me, Jean and Marian kiss us each on the cheeks, three times rather than the usual two. "*À toute à l'heure* ."

"*À toute à l'heure.*"

That night I roll over on my mattress trying not to disturb Marie who is, perhaps, accustomed to sharing her mattress with a total stranger. The goats coo in the barn. I feel lonely and worry, how long will the Fontaines want me, the inept city girl, working here? I don't know why I feel so drawn to this farm, this family, this land, but I am. There's something to learn here, something about life, about self-worth, and about growth. I'm determined to give this goatherd job my best shot.

The next morning, Michel and I scuttle to the barn. Again, I watch intently as he squeezes the teats and again, milk flows into the bucket. My turn. Gulp. I try to copy his example. I squeeze. I wiggle. I slide my fingers up and down. Still, no milk. Michel gestures for me to get up and takes the bucket abruptly, as though he's pissed. Forty minutes pass. He's milked thirty of the forty-two goats by himself. Tears form in the corner of my eyes.

Jacques, Camilla's husband, stands in the barn doorway, his feet planted like John Wayne, in his grey, baggy pants, tied at the waist with a rope. "It's time to take the goats out," I think he says.

Our motley crew of goats rubs against their partitions—some brown, some black, long hair, short hair, straight horns, curly horns. Twelve sheep, the color of dirty snow, cluster near the far wall. The cow looms like a matriarch in the back. Jacques unties the ropes, shooing the herd up the trail behind the barn. "*Allez!*" he shouts. "*Allez, Ma Rosa!*" he says to the cow.

The cloudless sky reflects the burning sun, so hot I'm panting behind Jacques and the goats as we hike up the hillside past mounds of sage and thyme. "You can pick some thyme," Jacques pantomimes. "We'll use it for tomorrow's stew." I nod, wiping the back of my neck.

Natasha, a scraggly, red-haired herd dog, part retriever, part one hundred other breeds, barks, dancing around us. Most of the goats trot to a group of short trees, barely taller than I, where they hoist up their legs and stretch their necks, chomping the leaves and nuts. A tiny caramel goat with stubby legs eats from broken limbs on the ground. Off to the side, the sheep nibble grass like they're glued together. The cow stands alone, whisking away flies with her tail.

Jacques and I sit on rocks overlooking the spectacular view. He chews a piece of straw, the color of his windswept hair, and points south, to where the white zigzags of the

Pyrenees Mountains spread over the horizon, dividing France and Spain and the little principality of Andorra. The 11,000-foot peaks rise like extended fingers, reaching from the earth toward the sky.

I don't believe in a patriarchal God, but I believe in something, and I am filled with that something's presence. The air and the earth and the goats and the great white Pyrenees' are all One. A soft breath washes over me, giving me an eloquent sense of belonging. The goats' bells ring like a Buddhist's call to meditation, and I believe with all my heart that I'm supposed to be here, which is weird, because I grew up in a city so, of course, I always thought I belonged in the city. But here, a feeling that has no words possesses me.

I'd love to show Garner this world. I think back on the first time we met in Eugene, Oregon, just one year ago, but it feels more like twenty. Dressed in jeans and a black tee shirt, he was so cute, kind of small, sitting comfortably on my friend Susannah's orange velour couch with a beer between his legs. "Hey," I said, as I came in the front door. He nodded at me while he fiddled with a Bic lighter, trying to smoke a joint.

I strolled to the kitchen where Susannah, her thick red hair tied back, boiled ramen noodles for dinner. "Who's that guy?" I asked, leaning against the counter, listening to the Grateful Dead sing *Truckin'* on the stereo.

"Garner. He lived in the same boarding house as Phil and me in Anchorage last year," she said. "He's visiting for awhile."

"Mmm," I said. "Cute." I grabbed a beer from the refrigerator, flipped off the cap, and returned to the living room, where I plopped on the couch next to him. "So you're from Alaska?" I asked, taking the joint he handed me.

"I work up on the rigs on the North Slope in winter," he said. "What's your story?"

I inhaled, then sipped my beer. "I'm still in college," I said. His tiny tattoo, Harley wings around a red heart, peeked from under his sleeve. His green eyes gleamed with a tint of grey, shining like polished stone.

"Ohhh. A college girl." He laughed with me, at himself, and seemed to get a kick out of anything. His skin was so pale and smooth it didn't fit such a rugged, street-smart kind of guy. Something about his wry wit, that shit-eating grin, made me smile. Soon enough, we were getting high, hanging out, getting high, going to movies, getting high. Here on the mountainside in France, I smile just thinking about him.

Jacques says something, I don't know what, but he points to the sun overhead, and I guess this is his way of telling time. "*Allez!*" Jacques calls. Natasha barks, circling the goats, nipping the ankles of the stragglers. The sheep, clumped together, trail behind like a giant wiggly worm.

When the goats are installed back in the barn, I head to "*La toilette*." Well, not exactly *"La toilette"* as in "bathroom." There's an outside curtain attached to the exterior of the house, which I push aside to see a splash of light shining on two planks across the middle of a half barrel. *"La toilette."*

I gingerly sit on the two boards and face, what? A sink? A shower? No, I face a rabbit cage two feet away with two black and white furry bunnies staring at me, twitching their noses as they munch their lettuce. I leave the stinky *"toilet"* as quickly as I can and again, gaze at the open hills of pastures and rocks and forest surrounding me on three sides. Beauty as I've never known before.

After our noon dinner, Jacques and I hike a different path with the goats. Again, I'm transported back to Garner and the day we sat on a bench at Skinner Butte Park. Such a simple scene—a spring day, the scent of rhododendrons just blooming, a boy and a girl in jeans holding hands, looking into each other's eyes. A cliché, really. But at twenty-five, I had never felt this way, so in love, so content, so excited and at peace at the same time. My first love, really. My first true love.

"You sigh a lot," he said.

I sighed. "Yeah," I said. But really, I was breathless. So this is what those love stories were all about. One year since I'd lost all that weight and here I was, in love, just like a fairy tale. I sighed again.

"Allez," calls Jacques. I jerk from daydreams, and stand, wiping dirt off my bottom. Clouds, white and fluffy, filter the pink and purple sky. Michel greets us at the barn. Time to try to milk again. Ugh! My enchanting high from being on the mountains drops like a New Years Eve ball. *Okay, I'll try again.* Michel settles on the pail once more and points as if to say, "Watch how my fingers move on the teats." I bend over and see him hold his thumb still. He squeezes down on

the front like he's squeezing toothpaste. I force a smile and trade places with him. I squeeze this way and that. I wiggle the teats. I take my hands away and stretch my fingers. I try again. Drip, drip, drip. I look in the pail. I listen. I try again. Drip, drip, drip.

Milk!!! What a grin Michel has. I feel like dancing and clapping. I did it! I, the city girl, learned to milk a goat.

Chapter Two

Randy

I finish milking that goat, and the next one, and the next, and soon the buckets fill to the brim. At evening supper, Marie, with her cheeks pink like a Renoir beauty, chatters in a tone which rises in excitement and falls in a hush, like she's telling us all scintillating gossip. Her younger brother, Louis, leaps up from his seat, spouting a retort. Marie argues back, squinting her eyes, scrunching her eyebrows.

Camilla smashes her fist on the table and yells at Marie, her hands flying, her voice growing louder, her eyes glaring in fury at whatever Marie said. I jump, startled, at attention, with no clue as to what's going on. It's like I'm watching a movie with no subtitles. "*Non, Mama,*" cries Marie, who grabs her glass and plate and runs to the kitchen. A second later the backdoor slams. What happened? Life on the farm is like wearing a veil. Everything is a wonder, a frosty blur, a guessing game. So far, guessing is fun. But, I am lonely, and I do miss my friends and family.

The wood in the fireplace sparks and crackles during our dinner of salad: lettuce, tomatoes, and carrots straight from their garden; goat's stew; and bread that's served at every meal. We act like Marie's outburst never happened, finishing our supper in silence. Louis leaves to feed food scraps to the chickens while Jacques pours another glass of wine, and perhaps another. The Languedoc wine, famous for being underrated, has a gentle tang, and costs far less than wine from Bordeaux or Provence. We drink wine instead of water, wine instead of milk, and then more wine just because it's wine.

After supper, Camilla pours the water from the cauldron into a dish bucket and I begin to wash the dirty glasses when a tall, poised woman with hair curled in a silver bun opens the door and enters, clicking her shoes on the hard cement. I guess knocking is overrated. She calls "*Camilla? Camilla?*" Camilla bounds in—she cannot walk without a hop to her step.

"*Ah, Bonjour! Bonjour, Madame Lyrrioone.*" Camilla wipes her hands on her apron.

The stranger, stiff as cardboard, speaks in a near monotone. Next to her, a boy who looks no more than thirteen, shifts from one leg to the other, bowing his head as if pondering the shape of his feet. The women converse. Did I hear, "This is Randy, your new goatherd?"

Are they planning to replace me? My heart pounds. Maybe this was a trial period, I failed, and they're going to send me on my way.

I scrub the pan harder. Won't they give me more of a chance? Sure, I don't know a thing about animals, and sure, my arms are too weak to carry the buckets, and yeah, I'm slow in the kitchen. But, still, the Fontaines act like they like me, at least Jacques and the children do. And, after all, I *can* milk a goat.

Dishes done, counter wiped, I squeeze past the visitors to toss out the dirty water in the field outside the door. I return to see the boy checking out the stark kitchen—the buckets in place of sinks, buckets in place of faucets, buckets in place of a garbage disposal. "Hello," he says to Camilla, in a voice just above a whisper. English! Like rain in the desert, the sound of English. I haven't heard any English since I left my cousin's a week ago. Now it rings like the sweetest sound in the universe. I'm so relieved and delighted. English! I now feel such compassion for all the immigrants in America whose second language is English. Because they have an accent, we imagine they're stupid. Oh, the joy of hearing my native language!

The water boils on the wood stove, rattling the metal lid. "Goodbye," Randy says to the woman in what sounds like a British accent. He speaks with no affection, no hug, no handshake. When the matron leaves, Camilla leads Randy up to the first loft, past Camilla's and Jacques' mattress, beyond the curtain to where his mattress lies on the floor next to Louis's and Michel's.

I dry the dishes, put them on a shelf, and adjourn to the *salle à manger* where I settle on the broad hearth, open my journal, put earphones in my ears, and turn on my cassette tape player.

"What are you listening to?" asks Marie.

"Oh, Marie! I didn't see you come in." I remove my earphones. I understand her simple words. "Mostly, rock n' roll."

"Really?" Marie's smile brightens. "What tapes do you have?"

"Let's see." We sort through the cassette tapes together. "Eric Clapton, The Stones, The Grateful Dead, Allman Brothers, Cat Stevens, Van Morrison. Oh, and here's John Prine, a favorite. And this is," I pull out a cassette. "Country. Waylon Jennings. Love it." She nods as though she recognizes most of the names.

"Ah. *Oui!* Can I listen?"

"Sure." I pull the earphones from the tape player and adjust the volume so everyone in the house can hear Mick Jagger sing *"SATISFACTION."*

"J'aime The Rolling Stones." Marie throws her hands to her cheeks, happy. We begin an unspoken arrangement. Camilla will buy the expensive batteries for the cassette player, and Marie and the family will use the tape recorder when I'm not listening to my tapes on the hills. The cost of batteries is an expensive downside to having no electrical outlets and only two dangling light bulbs in this entire house.

Randy strolls into the *salle à manger,* barely making a sound as he scans the blank walls, the *petit* dusty window, and the chest of drawers in the corner. Marie and Louis, seated at the table, chew on their pencils, their school books and papers spread out in front of them. At the other end of the table, Jacques slices leather into strips for a horse harness and rubs them with fragrant oil. Randy stands with his back to the fire, latching his hands behind him like a security guard. I close my journal, stick the pen in my pocket, and clear my throat. "Hi. I'm Elizabeth."

"Hi. Randy." He turns his thin face to me, reminding me of a bird, small and fragile.

"So," I ask, "What are you doing here?" I'm so excited to speak English, I can't hold it in any longer. He, however, does not appear to share the thrill.

A ray of moonlight slants onto his downy chin, his joyless eyes. "I've been living with my Mum's friend ever since I graduated from high school, a couple of months ago. Mum's friend knows Camilla and they decided this would be a nice place for me to be." My first eye opener: he's old enough to have graduated from high school?

"I lived on my father's farm, not far from Sydney," he says. "Both my brothers are horse jockeys, back in Australia." Oh—Australian. *That's* the beautiful accent. If being short and thin were all that mattered, he too could have been a jockey.

"I don't understand a word they're saying," he says, referring to the Fontaines. "I only studied German in school." His blond hair fluffs over his head, but the rest of his body is sharp—limbs that hang in angles, sea blue eyes that pierce, thin, tight lips that barely move when he speaks. "They showed me the barn. Disgusting." He nearly spits. "Those poor goats, all cramped together. Especially that poor pregnant cow. That barn is filthy."

"Ohhh. I like the Fontaines," I say, rubbing my chin. "I didn't even know Ma Rosa was pregnant. I've never been on a farm."

"What?" he says in horror. "You've never been on a farm?" As in, how is that possible? We're whispering even though no one can understand us.

"Well, no." I cross my arms. "I don't remember one, anyway. Except at county fairs. My prep school was way out in the countryside, but I spent my time on campus." I pick up a long stick from the hearth and poke the fire. The flames lash up under the hanging cauldron. "No, I'm a city girl."

"Never been on a farm," he says, shaking his head, dumbfounded.

Occasionally, Camilla asks Marie, who studies English in high school, "What are they saying?"

"I don't know."

Poor Marie is like me. She understands the simple words and phrases, but when it comes to native speakers in conversation, she's lost.

"What's the point of your English classes?" Camilla snaps. Obviously, there's no point whatsoever.

Randy and I are complete contrasts. I am average height with long, dark hair, chestnut eyes, and since I slimmed down two years ago, average weight. The carefree, broad-minded American, I like to see the "big picture," wondering about ethereal topics, universal truths, "the meaning of meaning." The downside is that I often skip the details.

Randy, blond, *petit,* and thin, is specific and particular, I can tell, listening to him describe the barn. "So you lived on a farm?" I ask.

"My whole life. Dad raises sheep and he's got about a thousand."

"You don't live with him?"

"Ay liz a bet a!" Camilla interrupts, excited. Camilla charges like the Energizer Bunny, always working; sometimes ecstatically happy, sometimes so mad that her tiny frame inflates like a parade balloon. Tonight, she's happy. Like charades, I try to guess what she's saying. "We're going somewhere? Tomorrow?" Camilla repeats and I guess again. "To look for chocolate?"

Early, before the sun begins its golden flight above the Pyrenees, Camilla and I hop into her little truck and drive for an hour, rumbling past several villages into a forest covered with blinding clumps of fog. Fresh, moist oak and moss smell rich and comforting as we drive through a den of trees, lit with patches of sun in miles and miles of forest. Camilla finally pulls over next to a grey dented car and parks. A short Frenchman holds a rope leash attached to a black, scruffy dog.

"Ay liz a bet a, il s'appelle Monsieur Pierre Rousseau."

"Bonjour," I say to the elderly man with broad cheeks wrinkled from weather and wind. He looks to be around seventy years old, but who can guess the age of someone who's lived life outdoors? His neck is thick, his hands gnarled like the roots of the trees, and he dresses in a worn brown coat and faded pants, thin at the knee. His dog, the size of a lab, wiggles his nose toward me, begging to be petted.

"Bonjour, Madame," he says to me.

"Mademoiselle," Camilla corrects.

"Ah, oui, et bonjour, Madame."

"Bonjour, Monsieur," Camilla says. Pretty formal for a friend. Who is this guy?

The dog whines, shakes his head, and heaves the old man's rope leash. "*Allez,*" Pierre says. Off we go, the dog leading, tugging the rope as he spurts ahead. He halts abruptly, smelling the root of a withered tree, and mashes his huge black paws into the ground, digging furiously. He freezes, lifts his head, and again, pulls Pierre forward. The dog drags Pierre, chased by Camilla, and I bring up the rear. What am I doing here? In these woods? In my life?

Into the deep forest we patter, over the soft carpet of dead leaves as the sun rises higher above us. The dog skids to a stop once again and, with his two paws in locomotive speed, he burrows, first with long, fast strokes, deeper and deeper into the ground.

"Arrête!" says Pierre, tugging the leash.

Camilla shouts to me, *"Maintenant!"* "Now!" She falls to her knees, reaching her gloved hand into the hole the dog started. I kneel beside Camilla, my knees cold and soaked, while she searches two inches into the ground, four inches, five inches, until she exclaims in excitement, *"Voilà!"* Raising it up like a trophy, she lifts a huge, ugly, black mushroom. Camilla beams like she's won the lottery while Pierre's deeply wrinkled face spreads into a proud, toothless smile.

Yuck! I hate mushrooms, and these seem particularly disgusting. I keep my thoughts to myself and force a smile. My knees and hands are freezing and damp and this is what we're doing all day? Following a dog in the mud? For mushrooms?

I'd gone mushroom hunting before, but it was nothing like this. In Eugene, Oregon, 'shrooming for psychedelics was a seasonal event. We didn't have dogs, of course, but one time, four years earlier, a group of us squeezed into a rusty Buick: my friend Susannah and I, her boyfriend, Joe, and their neighbors. I felt the zest I'd had as a child when we drove for hot, fresh maple syrup during sugaring off-season. The car puttered loudly to Venella, about twenty miles west of Eugene. "Joe knows someone who knows somebody," Susannah explained to me. "He knows of this farm with loads of cows."

That was what we were looking for—not cows exactly, but their dung. Joe parked the car, jumped a wire fence, and we followed. Brown cow pies scattered in mounds around the fenced pasture. Beige slender stalks, two inches high, topped with tiny heads like pointy flying saucers, sprouted from the dung. They clustered together like miniature trees. We carefully picked from the bottom of the stem, filling our paper bags with these magic mushrooms. The sky was a dusty blue and a small bird swooped overhead. A perfect day.

"RUN!" Joe's voice shattered the peace. He hollered again. "Run!" I heard a door slam as a farmer in overalls appeared on the porch of a white farmhouse, shotgun in hand.

"What the hell are you goddamn hippies doing?!" he yelled. Me? I was running like hell, pumping my legs as fast as I could, to reach the car before he shot that rifle. "Get off my property and stay off!"

Joe scrambled over the fence, Susannah followed, and I came up behind. A wire caught my jeans, scratched my leg, ripped my pants. I pulled, leaving a patch of denim, leaped in the car, and slammed the door. Joe smashed the accelerator and the car screeched, flying as fast as the old jalopy could go. Back at Susannah's, we each spread our 'shrooms like they were Halloween candy, counting, examining, categorizing our loot.

The next year, when 'shrooming season rolled around, Susannah said, "Things have changed."

"Oh?"

"You'll see," Susannah said, and smiled, her eyes blue and clear and sharp.

Once again, we piled into the cranky car, drove to the same field with the same cows, and the same farmhouse with peeling white paint. Joe and Susannah hopped the fence while I stood by the car, hesitating.

"No, really," she said. "Come on." A cow mooed from the other side of the field.

Sheesh, I thought, as I, too, climbed the fence and began picking the magic 'shrooms. When we filled our bags, Joe beckoned us. "Over here," he said.

I scratched my head as Joe marched up the front steps of the porch. "Susannah," I whispered, "What's he doing? He wants to get us all killed?"

"Watch," she said. Joe knocked on the door. I posed in my sprint position, ready to bolt.

The door creaked slowly open. I looked for the shotgun. The door opened farther. No gun. "Come on in." the farmer said.

Come on in? I thought. Are you kidding? In there?

"It's cool, Elizabeth." Susannah whispered. "Really."

I stepped slowly into the kitchen, torn linoleum covering the floor, faint scent of shrooms, and a small scale, like one used for grocery produce. "What's that?"

"It's a freeze dry machine," Susannah said in hushed voice.

"A what?"

"Shh."

I crossed my arms nervously. Micro-wave ovens had become popular around then, 1976. My friends and I thought they blasted radiation, though, and stayed away from them. And now here's a "freeze-dry machine" to contend with? What on earth is that?

"Give him your bag," said Joe. I handed over my precious 'shrooms. The farmer glanced inside the sack, weighed it, threw it on a shelf, and handed me a different bag; one stuffed with freeze-dried mushrooms.

What?

The farmer repeated the process for each of us, exchanging the fresh 'shrooms for the freeze-dried. Finally, he opened the door. "Nice doing business with you."

"You, too," said Joe. "Catch ya next year." And off we went, 'shrooms in hand, our private stash that would last all year.

Capitalism reigns, even here in the mushroom cow fields of Oregon.

Mushroom foraging is a treasure hunt, like a casino in nature, I decide, where we hope to win the prize. In France, with Camilla, Pierre, and his dog, I simply don't understand the stakes. As I hunker in those damp, dark woods, I'm lucky I don't speak more French because if I did, I would have embarrassed myself. After a full day in the forest, all I know is that my back aches, my knees shiver, and my nails ooze with mud.

Back home at the Fontaines, with my flashlight under my covers so not to wake Marie, I shuffle through the pages of my French-English dictionary. "T…truffles,'" I read. First definition, "chocolate candy," like I thought Camilla was saying the night before, and second, "the diamond of *haute cuisine,*" black truffles, the most valuable of all mushrooms, sold to exquisite Parisian restaurants for *$200 dollars a pound.* Ohhhh. That is the treasure we found.

Within a week, Randy and I follow a routine. One of us herds in the morning, while the other makes goat cheese, plucks chickens, mends clothes, sweeps the floor, helps Jacques move the portable fences for his horses, or performs a million other chores. We switch in the afternoon.

Every once in a while, we herd together. One day we hike to a grove of pigmy trees where our goats hover by our knees, singing their lovely goat songs, their tiny bells ringing across the hills. The white mountain peaks jut toward the cobalt sky and the beauty reminds me of Garner, a self-taught artist. He appears every night in my dreams, but I haven't heard from him since I left America. He'd be captivated by the specter of these Pyrenees looming on the horizon.

Garner lived with me off and on in Eugene, before he headed up to the oil fields in Alaska. I remember once when I left for my class, a Wittgenstein seminar, and he lay in bed asleep under rumbled sheets. My room was in shambles, like usual: clothes spread over the floor, piles in corners, sheets and blankets strewn everywhere, papers cluttering every bare inch of floor, books askew in my cinderblock bookcase, and plates from last night's dinner piled, unwashed.

When I came home from school, I opened my door and stopped. Gasped. Froze. Is this my room? My clothes were all neatly folded and put away. My rug, vacuumed. My bed, made with my pillow fluffed. All my books and papers aligned tidily in the bookcase, and the walls were decorated with my tennis racket hanging diagonally like a wall sculpture and Garner's incredible ink paintings pinned above my bed. This could be in *House and Gardens* magazine, if shabby chic were the style.

"Oh, my God, Garner. It's beautiful."

"Shh!" he said, embarrassed. "Don't tell anybody. I don't want them to think I'm good."

That's my bad ass Garner.

Now on this French hillside, goats huddle by Randy while I read *My Mother/Myself*, an insightful book about how women constantly carry their mother's messages inside their heads. Even though I've lived away from home for a decade, I still hear my Mom's words telling me what is proper and what is not. It's not proper to lunge across the table and grab a fistful of bread, that's for sure.

An hour later, I stuff my book in my pack. A tiny beige fellow with nubs that are barely horns, rubs against my legs. "*Allez!*" Randy and I call. Natasha and our other herd dog, mangy, black-and-white Frippo, leap around us, nipping the goats, sheep, and the cow, and we all move on.

At the next spot, Randy scratches a goat's head between the horns. "You never said how you came to be here," he says.

Well, you never asked, I think. Randy seldom pays attention to me. First and foremost are the animals. I reflect on the long series of events that led me here. I could go back to second grade when I wrote my first play. And of course, what writer doesn't want to go to Paris? But, in reality, I'd probably never be here if it weren't for Garner.

I wasn't sure how much I wanted to tell Randy. I didn't want to tell him that I used to be fat, which was, in some ways, like wearing protective armor. I didn't want to tell him about falling in love with Garner just before I graduated in December of 1979, about taking a cocktail waitress job over the winter while Garner worked on the North Slope in the Arctic, about anxiously waiting for him, building my life around his, at least in my dreams.

I surely didn't want to tell him about a night at MacKenzie's bar, when I scooted past a dart champion balancing my tray of beers, gin, and tequila. The dart player squinted, aimed, and tossed a bull's-eye. "*Yes!*" he screamed, punching the air, dancing a crude jig. A woman with orange powder makeup hunched over the bar, clinked ice cubes in her glass, and listened to *Dust in the Wind* on the jukebox. I handed Jim, a "regular," his rum and coke.

Susannah waited for me in a vinyl booth, covered with a sticky film. "I can only sit a minute," I said, slipping in across from her, brushing away the thick cigarette smoke.

"What do you hear from Garner?" She twisted her red hair into a bun.

"Next week. He's supposed to be here May fifteenth." My stomach tingled. "I can't wait."

Susannah crossed her arms, her turquoise eyes set on mine. "Be careful," she said.

"Be careful?"

"You know what I mean." She'd known Garner in Alaska and thought he'd mess with my heart. He was, after all, my first true love—the first man I'd been with since I'd lost sixty pounds.

On a misty day the following week, I offered Mr. Gin and Tonic his extra lime when MacKenzie's door suddenly banged open. Garner swaggered in, a grin painted on his face, his green eyes blazing with coke. I raced to him, arms outstretched, tears rolling like a romantic movie.

Our first days, we bubbled with love. With a pug nose and wry smile, his face looked boyish. He smelled fresh, such a contradiction from his biker stories, riding with the Hell's Angels. I thought he grew up in New York's gangs, but I could never pin him down. "I'm not big," he once said, "but, I'm fast." And vicious. A mean fighter. Whom I adored.

By his third day home, our conversations faltered. A canyon gapped between us. Being madly in love felt like a memory, faint, impossible to grasp. "Let's go to the beach," I said. "Get out of town." Get back to the way we were, I thought.

We hitchhiked from Eugene to Florence, where sand dunes billowed for miles on the Oregon coast. We rented a room at the Motel 6. Unlocking our door, Garner dove onto the bed, turned up the TV, and opened a quart bottle of Olympia beer.

"Don't you want to walk on the beach?"

"In that rain? Man, do you know how long it's been since I've seen TV? Watched a game?"

I snatched my raincoat and dragged myself alone to the beach, where waves slapped their white heads, plowing toward shore, and the mist clung to my face. I had cherished Garner's letters from Alaska, and I'd imagined us living together, maybe forever. But now? Now, I felt hollow, drained, empty. I smelled the damp salt air. Was our love just alcohol and sex? Our laughter just the drugs? My feet sunk into the wet sand. How can we get back to the way we were? Back to his first day home? Have I wasted five months of my life waiting for him?

Gusts of wind whooshed behind me and banged the motel room door as I entered to the stench of cigarettes and beer, the blaring television, and Garner still on his stomach on the bed, his head and chin propped on his hands. I breezed past him to towel dry my hair in the bathroom. "I'm going to Utah for the summer," he yelled through the closed door. "Come with me."

“What?!” My voice sounded like an owl’s screech. I threw open the bathroom door. "Utah?!” I pictured brown plains and plateaus like piles of pancakes, with a huddle of trailers in tiny rows, sun and heat pounding against their tin roofs. Garner would go to work at dawn, I imagined, while I’d wait for him. I’d eat, watch TV, and stand in the doorway like a scene from the dustbowl. I could hear the ripped screen flapping against the thin metal siding. The days would repeat themselves, one after another, each in unison, each in misery.

Water dripped from my hair onto the bed. “What would I do in Utah?” I asked. “I’d be miserable, waiting for you every day in a trailer. I’ve been waiting for you for months, and now you’re going again?” Tears streamed down face. “What would I do there? Nothing!” I felt my world slipping in front of me, plunging, shattered.

Back in MacKenzie’s a week later, the juke box blasted. Susannah lit a cigarette and I wiped my eyes once more. “He’s going to Utah?” Susannah asked. “Why Utah?”

“Oil drills.” I sipped my Grand Marnier. “Another job to look for oil. And I don’t want to stand around a fuckin’ trailer park, waiting for him to come home.” A pool stick shot an eight ball behind us. “Besides, it wasn’t the same between us. The first days were magic, but after that, we crumbled. We had nothing to talk about.” My stomach felt raw. The air reeked of cigarettes. “I don’t know what happened to our dreams of being together.”

Susannah tapped her Marlboro on the plastic ashtray. “Sweetie, it’s good you’re not going to Utah."

"What am I going to do?" For the tenth time that night *Dust in the Wind* crooned on the jukebox. "I need to go somewhere." I said. "Anywhere. I've just been killing time, doing nothing but waiting for him!"

Susannah's eyebrows pressed together.

"What should I do? I'm a college graduate now. I've got to do something. Where should I go?"

Never once did I imagine herding goats in the mountains of the South of France. Instead, I cried for an hour.

A week later, with Johnny Paycheck singing "Take This Job and Shove It" in the background, I approached my boss. "I quit," I said, and sailed from the smoky bar never to return.

"Well?" said Randy. I snapped out of my daydream. "I just wondered how you happened to be here." Dressed in his faded, blue sweatshirt, well-worn jeans, and practical, black boots, he looked like he fit on this hillside, a true goatherd with his hand of nuts open for the goats to nibble.

I continued reflecting, not saying a word. After I quit my job, I needed to muse, sort out my life, figure out what to do. I boarded a train to Mt. Shasta to meditate for a week at a Zen Buddhist Abbey. In a large hall reminiscent of a barn, I sat among monks and novices and visitors, trying to balance the tip of my spine on a hard black pillow, practicing Zazen in the Soto Zen method of meditation. Sandalwood incense fogged the air. At home I'd meditated sitting straight, legs down, on in a chair, saying a mantra over and over in my head. Anyone can do that. With Zazen, I was supposed to sit cross legged and "not think; just sit," gently focusing on the center of my forehead. "Let your thoughts go," I was told. "Pay attention to your thoughts, but don't get caught up in them." That was easier said than done. I'd meditated for eight years, so I thought, *no problem.* Yeah, problem. Big problem. All these monks are probably "not thinking" about God and spirit and stuff, I thought. All I could "not think" about was Garner.

While Garner was in Alaska, I'd attended a workshop in Eugene for people who loved people who drank too much. That was Garner through and through. "You need to let your loved one live his own life," the workshop leader taught. "Maybe he'll change, maybe not. Let go with love. Keep your boundaries. Respond, don't react. Believe in yourself.'"

Believe in myself? What does that mean? Breaking the Abbey's rule of "silence at all times," another visitor and I whispered as we weeded in the garden. "Some women," she said, "go into any room with three hundred people and are attracted to the one and only alcoholic." That was me.

Garner had been my own James Dean. He preferred trudging through dark alleys to walking on the streets. He hated "nice"—people who were "nice," words that were "nice." That spelled hypocrisy to him. I couldn't explain my obsession with Garner, not even to myself. Who can rationalize a first love? Especially for a formerly obese woman at my age? He'd consumed me, and when we fell apart, I felt lost, like a pebble tossed in a pool, sinking. Slowly sinking.

I remembered my lifelong dream of being a writer in Paris. I had friends in Europe, plus a distant cousin. Yes, that's what I would do. Go to Europe. I packed my bags. From the Abbey I moved to St Louis with my sister and her husband, where I worked in a Chinese restaurant for the summer. From there, I went home, to my parents in Massachusetts.

"I'm going to Europe," I told my mom and dad.

"Europe? By yourself? Ohhh, honey." They were none too pleased, but they helped me get ready and drove me to Logan airport.

Landing at Heathrow in London, I felt like Alice in Wonderland. Completely baffled. The world was the same, and yet entirely different. I needed to call my old roommate Karen, who had offered me her couch for the week. I found a phone booth and emptied a pocketful of coins into my palms. What's a half-pence? What's a shilling?

I clutched Karen's phone number on a sheet of paper as announcements about arrivals and departures boomed through the airport. Do I dial first? Put the coins in first? Which ones? The telephone cord twisted around me and the coins stuck to my sweaty palm. I dropped in the silver, listening to the clinking sounds. Like a miracle, Karen's voice came through the line. Yay! Karen!

"Just take the tube," Karen said. "I'll meet you at my station."

"The tube?" What the hell is a tube?

I caught up with Karen whom I hadn't seen in a year. I befriended a man quite enamored with me, toured the London sights, and then bussed and ferried to Paris.

In the City of Light, I once again faced my nemesis: the phone booth. I struggled with my francs in one pocket, my English crowns in another, and American quarters in a third. I put coins in slots, heard some indecipherable voices, and hung up. Eight years had passed since I studied French, my worst subject. At least in London, they spoke English. I tried again, sifting through my coins, dropping them in. School children prattled by in their blue uniforms and backpacks. (Backpacks for school books. What a clever idea! We should try that in America, I thought.) Many hours and tears later, I heard a familiar voice.

"Dory?"

"Yes."

"This is Elizabeth! Elizabeth Corcoran!" Dory, with whom I'd gone from nursery school through prep school, hadn't seen or heard from me in ten years. Now, married with two children, Dory had lived in Paris since being an *au pair* right after college.

"Are you in your hotel?" she asked.

Are you kidding? I could barely make a phone call! Hotel? What hotel?

"Give me a call when you get settled and we can get together for coffee."

Clearly, a kind and gracious response from someone I hadn't spoken to in a decade. Still, I'd hoped she'd say, "Come on over and stay." I muttered something and she said, "Sometimes it takes a leap of faith." Well, I was surely leaping.

I circled the *rue de* this and the *rue de* that until I finally discovered a hotel in my already frayed "Let's Go France" guidebook. The fine Parisian establishment, "Hotel California," offered a clean bed where I slept undisturbed for fifteen hours.

I drank coffee with my friend at her high rise apartment while her children attended school. Dory was clearly settled into Parisian life. Married to a pilot, she flew back and forth across the Atlantic like it was the Connecticut River. As I strolled out the lobby door after our visit, I sighed. Such a different world. I wondered if I had wasted the last ten years of my life.

I explored the Left Bank, the Right Bank, the museums, and the bookstores. I inhaled the sweet scent of crêpes bubbling with lemon and chocolate and fresh whipped cream. But I couldn't figure out any way to actually live in Paris, so instead I migrated south.

Randy pets a black goat, waiting for my answer. "How did I get here?" I say. "Well, I graduated from college, broke up with a guy, and visited a cousin who knew Camilla."

"Ah," he says. That's enough for him. He turns to his goat. "This guy's name will be Harrison. See how much longer his hair is than anyone else's? 'Hairy Harrison.'" The toffee-colored doe licks Randy's hands, nuzzling, trying to get to the nuts he picked off the ground.

Silver clouds float overhead. Wild sage infuses the air. I haul out my tape recorder, my French lesson cassette tape, and its accompanying language book that I bought in Paris. Hopefully, if I listen to the tape, and follow along with the corresponding chapter in the book, I'll learn the French I didn't learn in school. I repeat the lesson in chapter three: "The woman entered the store to buy some cheese." A fly buzzes, tickling my nose.

Here's irony: even though French was my worst subject, I performed so well on my French Achievement Tests in high school that I was exempt from the foreign language requirement in college. Lot of good that did me.

While I study, Randy converses with the goats, waggling their long ears. "And this is Chinny," he says to me, or to himself, or to Chinny, I'm not sure which. "Look at your weird beard over your chin."

A *petit chevre* taps his feet on a rock next to me, and curls around my knees. I regard my book, eye the goat, and then the book again. Finally, I flip off the tape recorder and pet the tiny fellow. "This guy's my favorite," I say. "Let's call him 'Baby.'"

"This is Georgia," Randy says. "Look at his ankle! It's still bruised from Frippo's bite yesterday." Nope, I didn't notice the bruise. "These dogs are awful. I'll never use them. They're vicious."

Yikes, I think. I don't think I could herd without the dogs. They're my saviors. When I'm reading my books, and the goats scatter out of sight, I simply call the dogs and *voila*, they all appear. Frippo rolls over on his back, begging me to rub his white-patched stomach. Natasha rests her long nose between her two paws and exhales a pathetic dog sigh.

"You've got to quit chewing on these goats!" I say, "Can't you just 'nudge' them a little?"

Copying Randy, who is my teacher in all things goat, I pluck some leaves off a branch for a copper-colored critter. "Let's name this one, 'Elusive,'" I say. "She reminds me of a cat, acting like 'ohhhh, you're not important to me,' but she's always there—just six or eight feet away. And this one, she's 'Split-Infinitive,'" I say of a goat whose horns look split and crooked.

Baby, Elusive, and Split-Infinitive break through my shell. I've been so focused on reading, meditating, and thinking about Garner, that I've missed out on the goats. I still don't care about the sheep, though. They have no personalities. The sheep flock together like barnacles, super skittish, and we don't have names for any them. And the cow? "Ma Rosa" meanders behind, ignoring us as much as possible.

Baby and I lag behind as Randy and the stream of animals tramp onward to a third spot. Charlie halts mid-step and turns, plowing into Baby, heaving her into the trees. "Stop that! Scoot!" I swat Charlie. "Come here, Baby." I lead her out of the trees, back to the trail where she runs as fast as her little legs will go, trying to catch up with the rest of the herd.

"Hey, Randy. Come check it out." I point down into the valley. "Look at those old ruins. Wouldn't it be fun to explore some day?" If I understand Jacques correctly, this land belongs to the government for use by families who live in the region. Each family has a multi-acre area for animals to graze. Over the months, we'll rotate through different sections of land, so the animals will have fresh grass and trees throughout the year.

“You know, Randy,” I say, “I’m so glad we can herd together.” He glances sideways at me, his lips pressed together. Is that a smile?

It’s not that I don’t like herding alone—I do. Growing up, one sister started college when I began kindergarten, and I rarely played with the other, three years older than I. I’ve always enjoyed being by myself. However, not being able to communicate in English before Randy joined the family brought such a keen sense of isolation and deep loneliness that being with him is utter joy.

“It’s weird not having friends here," I say. "Camilla’s not like a friend. She’s my boss." I scratch Baby's chin. "You know, I’d really like to be friends with Marian. I mean, she and Jean stop by every other day, she’s about my age, and she’s so gorgeous.” Randy feeds nuts to one of the smaller goats. “But neither of us understands a word the other says. It’s such a bummer. We just don’t understand each other at all.”

Randy tears leaves from a tree for Chinny. I never really understood what “taciturn” meant before, but now I do. It means Randy: quiet, distant, reticent. He’s so unlike me, the effusive American, who wants everyone to like her, excited by life, most of the time. Randy’s lips squish together like a prissy old teacher. He knows all about animals, and since I don’t know how the Fontaines can afford two goatherds, I worry more about getting fired. If they can't afford running water, how can they afford two goatherds? "You’ll catch on," *petit* Randy reassures me.

At our new herding spot, I perch on a rock and empty my pack once more. My free-spirited wanderlust seems to be transforming, and the loose threads of my life—the rigid New England heritage, the kindness and non-judgmental nature of my Ohio friends, the laid-back Oregonian lifestyle—all are fusing together, integrating. Randy points to the goats around him, one by one. "I like you. I like you. I don't like you. I like you. I don't like you," he says.

"Randy, you are so definitive," I say. "So clear on whom you like and don't like." But what I really think is, *they're goats, for God's sake.*

But to Randy, the goats are equal, if not more important, than humans. His opinions are solid, straightforward, and unwavering—unlike me, who's so wishy-washy, just like Charlie Brown. What I like, what I don't like, how I feel, what's okay, what isn't okay—it's all muddled. I envy Randy's clarity.

That night, I toss and turn in bed. Or, more accurately, on my shared mattress on the floor. It's been ten years since I lived under my parents' roof, but now I miss them more than ever. I miss my mom most, who had three (four, actually—one died in infancy) children over sixteen years and barely had a life outside of parenting. I'm gaining insight reading *My Mother/Myself.* Mom coddled me, the youngest. Thus, my rebellion, my extra strong fight for independence. She tried, certainly: PTA, Girls Scouts, Altar Guild at church, President of the Junior League. She almost died once, and that's what I remember as I lie in the French loft listening to the gentle snores from the mattress below.

At age fifteen, when I was a student at MacDuffie School for Girls, I stood next to her bed in the ICU. She lay still, unmoving, a lock curled on her forehead, her face white and drawn with tubes reaching into her nose, out her veins. Skinny. She seemed so skinny.

I remember the wretched stench of antiseptic. The beeping of the machines. Beep. Beep. Beep. I held my tears, terrified. I'd never felt such fear. I didn't know what was wrong, why she was so sick. Some sort of strange virus?

I could talk to no one. My sisters, my father—we didn't speak about emotions. My friends from the neighborhood? They were in different worlds—different prep schools or the public high school.

At my private girls' school, study was king, and lunchtime, our only social time. I didn't say between bites of mac 'n cheese, *I'm afraid that my mom is dying.* I didn't say when I gulped my milk, *I don't think the doctors know what's wrong.* Mom stayed in the ICU for an entire month, and I was so scared that I'd cry all day if I talked about her. No, I didn't talk about my mom at lunch. What I said instead was, "What did you think about that Latin test?"

I began to overeat compulsively in junior high, but when my Mom nearly died, it exploded. Instead of talking, I ate. Instead of crying, I ate. Instead of being mad, I ate. Food consumed me. My life became a battle to eat, to not eat. Starve with Carnation Slender at lunch, binge on Friendly's coffee ice cream at night. Any confidence, or sense of worth I might have had, vanished. Obsession overtook me. I binged on food I didn't even like. I just ate.

My Mom lived, and I began to relax, but I still ate. And dieted. And ate some more.

On our French farm, October chills replace the brutal September heat. One October morning Camilla tells me, "*Ay liz a bet a,* wash the forms, and we'll make cheese." Though I understand more words and phrases than I did in the beginning, we've also become excellent at pantomime. I carry the empty buckets to the water truck outside, where powder puff clouds drift over the snowy mountain peaks. I'm still enchanted by the nature surrounding me, but it sure would be nice to have some fun. I'm stronger now, and can carry two buckets completely filled. In fact, I've never been this strong. Still, I miss my friends in Eugene. I miss partying, dancing, concerts—getting wild and having fun. I used to go to concerts—Watkins Glen, the largest concert ever, bigger than Woodstock; Grateful Dead concerts every year since 1972; music on all the stages at the Oregon Country Faire, along with the Karamazov Brothers juggling naked for the midnight show. I've lived here five weeks, and I'm getting restless.

When water in the cauldron boils, I pour it into the washing bucket and begin to scrub the little draining holes in the dozens of plastic cylinders called "forms" that we use for making cheese. "Ok," says Camilla. "Time to make *fromage de chèvre.*"

We cook milk over the wood stove in the kitchen, and add whey for thickening. "*Maintenant,*" Camilla demonstrates. "Pour the cheese mixture into the straining cups, the 'forms'."

I follow her instructions. The cheese sits in the "forms" overnight. The next day, we pour the mixture into freshly cleaned forms and strain them again. Over the next couple of days, the process is repeated until the cheese thickens into firm mounds.

We transfer the strained mounds into the *fromagerie,* and place them on shelves of metal netting that look like window screens. Cheese mounds fill all the shelves. The freshest cheese is about three inches in diameter and an inch tall, but the longer it dries, the more it shrinks. The taste intensifies. Cheese that dries one week is relatively soft and bland, while cheese dried for five months grows an ugly green-blue coat of mold on the outside, which we scrape off. This cheese tastes sharp, almost bitter, and, like wine, it's valued for its age.

I emerge from the *fromagerie* just as Randy is hanging his coat on the hook by the kitchen door. "That Ma Rosa's getting ornery," he says. "She wants to stand like a statue all day. She's due in December, by the size of her. Most of the female goats are pregnant, too. There'll be quite a few births in spring." I love Randy's Australian lilt when he says, "quite a few."

"I need to call the dogs to get Ma Rosa to follow the herd," I say. "She is so damn stubborn. She drives me crazy!" The silverware jingles as I set the table. I carry the salad out to the *salle à manger*. "By the way, Michel is back."

Randy rubs his hands together, trying to warm himself by the fire. "Where's he been?"

"I haven't a clue," I say, using one of Randy's favorite phrases. "Here one second, gone the next. I don't know when he comes or where he goes, and I never understand anything he says."

At noon dinner, no one speaks. The Fontaines listen to their daily soap opera, *Louisianne,* on the radio. The story, about a French family in Louisiana during the late seventeen hundreds, progresses through history. Now, we're at around 1800, Camilla explains, the time before Napoleon sells the French territory to Thomas Jefferson. Unfortunately, like most of the talk radio, I understand next to none.

When today's episode finishes, I throw my pack over my shoulder, and head to the door.

"Joyeux Anniversaire," Michel says to his parents.

I turn. "Your anniversary? You should celebrate! Go dancing." The family understands my simple sentences.

Camilla stirs the wood in the fireplace, blowing on the embers to ignite the fitful flames. "Would you like to go to a dance?" she asks me. Have I heard correctly? *Une danse? Vraiment?* Really?

Absolument!

Chapter Three

The Dance

I'm tickled to death. *OUI! Une danse!* The only time I've left the house in five weeks was to go mushroom hunting. My whole world is the Fontaines, Randy, and Marian and Jean. I love to dance.

Randy accompanies me to the barn. It feels rude to speak English in front of the Fontaines since they don't understand anything we say. "Do they have dances with the whole family in Australia?"

"Well, I guess not," Randy says. "I don't really go to dances."

I creak open the barn door, and he helps me unfasten the rope partitions that separate the goats. "Teenagers in America never dance with their parents. I mean, I like rock n'roll, and some of my friends like disco. But people my parents' age? I don't know what they do. Waltz? Whatever, no kid ever dances with their parents."

"See you later, Randy! *Allez, allez,*" I call to my goats. I'm thrilled—and curious—about the dance.

As a teenager and in my early twenties, I shied away from dancing. I was too fat. I didn't want people to see all the flab bouncing up and down. Worse than that—my body was stiff as steel. Zero flexibility.

Even in elementary school, I used to squirm when John or Ruth picked the kickball teams. *Oh, please, let me not be the very last.* Thank God for Karen Kower. She was picked last. I was second to last. But such torture, hearing the names called out for teams. *Pick me. Please pick me.* I wasn't even fat. Chubby, maybe, but not like I was in high school when I wasn't invited to a single dance or prom; when I suddenly had my period every time I was supposed to be in gym class. Didn't the school nurses wonder how a girl can have her period every two weeks? Didn't they figure out that some girls would do anything to get out of looking foolish in PE?

My first dance after I lost sixty pounds was with Garner on Halloween. We danced all night at a community center to a band playing Grateful Dead songs. I wore the black taffeta dress I found in the free box at White Bird, the crisis clinic where I volunteered. It plunged at the neckline and clung to my newly carved waist. I felt more beautiful than I ever had before. Gorgeous. Hot. We danced and swirled in the pot-scented hall, drank beers, and danced some more. Back at Susannah's, we passed out in our clothes. In the morning, Garner rolled over to kiss me. "Yuck!" I said. "You smell like dead beer!"

"Dead Beer?" he said. "That's my new name."

And I was even more in love. Thinking back on this, I roll my eyes. How did I ever get so smitten?

The barn door slides shut behind me and my herd skips ahead. "Come on Elusive, let's go." Love is not rational, but next time, *next time* I'm attracted to a guy, I'm going to pay attention with my *head.* I'm not going to let myself fall for someone who's no good for me; not going to pick some guy with a beautiful heart who just can't get it together. Garner, I wish I'd never fallen for you.

On the long awaited day of the dance, Marie holds up two scarves and asks me, "*Ay liz a bet a,* do you like the blue or the red?"

"Umm." I smell the sweet carrot soup on the stove. "Show me. Put them up to your face." Marie rubs them on her cheeks, lovely, yet innocent. "The rose one," I say. "You'll be beautiful." She circles the scarf around her neck, and, with the low neckline of her flowered blouse and thin gold necklace, she is lovely. As for myself, I don't have to choose. I have only one outfit: the long maroon skirt I wore hitchhiking from Paris.

Marie and I take turns heating the heavy, old-fashioned iron on the wood stove, and ironing our clothes on the table. She plants herself in front of the only mirror in the house, eight by six inches, hanging from a nail on the trusses near her parents' mattress. With her mother's brush, Marie lifts her auburn locks, brushes underneath, leaving her hair down, slightly tossed. She dabs blush on her cheeks, runs red lipstick over her lips, and carefully applies her mascara. When Camilla sees her daughter, she barks some harsh words. Marie shines, appearing more like nineteen years old than fourteen—which is probably what irritated her mother. But Camilla's annoyance dissolves quickly as she dons a light-blue cashmere sweater I've never seen. Bubbling, Camilla waves her hands, pushes her glasses up her nose, and chatters happily like she drank ten coffees. What is she saying? I haven't a clue.

Jacques and Randy, on the other hand, express nothing—they don't change their clothes or even smile. They merely wait for the contingent of women. I'm guessing that Louis, at eleven, anticipates staying up late. And Michel? He probably hopes the international hope of every seventeen-year-old boy, "Will I get lucky?"

We all squeeze into the little truck and sputter along, forking past the cluster of stone houses where we purchase our monthly vat of wine. Heading up a bumpy road under a deep blue, violet-streaked sky, the wet earth and sage smell sweet and vibrant. Jacques drives over a hill, down into a valley, and parks near the stone houses which line each side of the road. Tumbling out of the car, the women straighten their hair and blouses for their entrance to the uninviting cement building, a dance hall for the night.

Camilla leads, followed by Jacques, the rest of us trailing, cowering together as though to hide from the masses. And there are masses. Old people, young people, tall, short, with teeth and toothless, ragged and styled, gather in a festive jubilation such as I've seldom seen. The room feels homey, like an American Grange Hall. One wall is lined with tables of cheese, crackers, salami, and precious olives. At one end of the room, a DJ fiddles with the record player and speakers. Camilla kisses the cheeks of old friends, Jacques moves to chat with the men, and the children scatter to find their school mates.

Randy and I huddle together by the food table as if we're a couple. "There's Marian," I point out to Randy. The slender, golden woman with the famous apple-skin-flicking skills leans against the wall by herself. "I'm going to try to speak to her," I declare. Randy is expressionless. "Wish me luck." I picture Randy like a cantankerous old gentleman at a London men's club, harping on the woes of the world, lounging in a tall armchair with a tight collar and cigar.

"Bonjour, Marian," I say.

"*Ah, bonjour, Ay liz a bet a.*" She kisses me on each cheek, once, twice. I twirl my hair behind my ear, awkward. God, I really want to befriend her. She moves so gracefully, even in her overly large, grey sweater that hangs from her bony shoulders. Our conversation falters.

Marian and Jean visit the farm several times a week, so I've spent quite a bit of time with her, but still, I know little about her. She lives in a village up the road, but does she have animals? And how do they make money living out here? Her smile seems forced, her eyes sad, her face framed in melancholy.

I say that I am excited to be at the dance and she responds with something I don't understand. I am stumped on how to reply. Our language barrier is like the Berlin Wall. "Well, nice to see you. Have fun! *A tout a' l'heure.*" I kiss her cheeks and wander back to Randy.

"It's so frustrating," I say to him. "Marian seems like a gentle soul, but it's so hard to talk with her."

Randy doesn't answer. Sometimes I wonder if the only relationships that matter to him are with the goats. He's no people person, that's for sure. He says more often than not,

"I could care less." And usually, that's when we're talking about Camilla or Jacques or Marie.

The room hushes. "Randy, do you think they'll play something like *Au Claire de la Lune,* songs we learned in school?" He shrugs, as indifferent as I am enthusiastic.

The DJ, who looks about thirty, with a stubble of hair on his chin, announces, "Time to begin." Okay, what will it be? Couples and groups of women sashay to the center of the room, laughing, holding hands, wiggling.

I'm so excited to dance. My body is awakening. I spent most of life my sitting—in front of books or TV or the refrigerator, but since I've been at the farm, electricity burns within me as my body changes, comes to life. I'm stronger than ever. Every day, when I herd the goats, climb the hills, and carry water, my legs and arms and shoulders perk up as though they've been in a deep sleep.

And now, I'm ready to free that energy and dance the night away. I can't wait for the music to start. What's it going to be for this group—French farmers and children and grandparents all mixed together?

The DJ lifts the record player needle, and carefully places it on the record. I smell garlic snacks and Languedoc wine as the air stills, suspended in silence. What will it be? We wait.

Suddenly, Eric Clapton blasts, *"If you want to hang out, you've got to take her out…COCAINE."* In English! Here, in this ancient village, hidden in the depths of the French mountains of Languedoc, Eric Clapton screams, *"If you want to get down, get down on the ground…"*

I jump, spin, throw out my arm and sing out loud, *"Cocaine!"* Finally, finally, after weeks in this foreign world, they are playing my songs, my music, my language. I feel I've been to the moon and returned home, hearing these songs I know and love.

Girls and women jam the dance floor, shaking their buns, twisting, contorting, bopping all around. Like at a high school dance, men talk and drink and watch the women. Camilla, one of the first on the floor, reaches for my hand. "*Viens*," she says. "Come with me." I twirl, spreading my arms as I sing out loud, transported to another place and time which is my world, which is good ole' rock and roll.

Eric Clapton is followed by the Allman Brothers, Jethro Tull, the Rolling Stones, the Beatles, Creedence Clearwater Revival—all my college albums. In all the world of songs and dances, this belongs to me. I hop until my feet are sore, my forehead soaked, and my mouth dry.

After an intermission, the room becomes quiet, calm, and almost somber. I sip wine and nibble cheese as I catch my breath, smelling the sweet sweat that fills the room. This may be the way soldiers feel when the USO, a touch of home, comes to entertain.

The DJ falls back into his chair, crosses his arms, and nods to a stooped farmer with a creased face, who stands, hobbles with his accordion to the middle of the room. His fingers stroke the keys, he squeezes the ancient instrument, and the silence breaks into the most beautiful ballad I've ever heard, like in movies set in World War II Vichy France.

Women with white hair tucked under their red bandanas, tied around their chins, smile as they press their hands together, perhaps remembering the good and the bad times gone by. I survey all the families. Children, teenagers, parents, grandparents, mingle together, grateful for this wonderful celebration of what, I will never know.

Chapter Four

Another Brick in the Wall

With aching legs after my wild night of dancing, I wake with a grin plastered on my face. I curl up under my blankets, listening to Camilla and Marie holler at each other in the kitchen below. A door bangs and someone stomps out. Pots rattle. Pans clang. I picture Camilla scouring the dishes until they shine like diamonds, furious about something Marie did or said. I drag myself out of bed, pitying the mother and daughter who scream and fight almost every day. The madder Camilla becomes, the more Marie whines and acts like a brat. But when I think about last night's dance, I glow. It was the most fun I've had since I moved to the farm.

In the morning on the hills with my herd, I sing "*I see the needle and the damage done…*," a song Susannah and I sang when we hitchhiked Highway 101 on the California coast. I can't carry a tune, but my goats don't care. They trot over to their little trees, Georgia, Split-Infinitive, and Jam squeezing out the little ones. I pick up a branch with leaves and nuts for Baby who snuggles right next to me, chomping away, and for Elusive, who lingers to the side as usual. Elusive acts like she's wearing an electric fence collar: she won't come closer than an eight-foot radius of me. But, she never wanders too far, either. Always close, but not *too* close.

Is that Garner's story, too? The idea of being close to me sounded good when he worked in Alaska, but when he got too close, he ran to Utah? Baby climbs all over me. If she were a cat, she'd be purring, but instead she's cooing a sweet goat song.

When Elusive chews leaves from the branch I extend to her, she reminds me of Antoine de Saint-Exupéry's *The Little Prince*. Maybe I can tame Elusive like the little prince tamed his rose. Maybe I can tame Garner. But, maybe I can't. And maybe I shouldn't even try.

We wander through swaths of sage along the trails, and I sing songs from church hymns to Janis Joplin to camp songs, Stephen Foster and Woody Guthrie. At the next cluster of trees, I slip my pack under my head and sleep soundly like Little Boy Blue. Yes, my life is like a nursery rhyme—that's the only way to describe it. When I wake, Baby is sleeping next to me. I sit up on a flat rock and read spiritual writings, Buddhist and Christian, then mediate and pray—my daily routine. Prayer for me is the great mystery, the unexplainable mystery. Mostly, my prayers are those of gratitude.

Back at the house, voices shout on the radio. "America! America!" Jimmy Carter and Ronald Reagan are fighting it out for the American presidency. Carter has the lead. Phew! The French sure must have strong opinions, because they talk about the American elections all the time, with vehemence and passion. What they're barking on the radio, though, I have no idea.

In the middle of our supper of bread, milk, and jam—I've long since become accustomed to the fact that bread, milk, and jam are our supper each and every Thursday night—our neighbor, whom I call Mr. Bawdy, bursts in like a firestorm. Out of our enormous four-house village, only two houses are occupied during the fall and winter. The other two are summer houses for city folk. Bawdy wears his shirt half-buttoned over his hairy chest and protruding pudgy belly. Loud, boisterous, and dirty, he's crude. He's rude. And his hair looks dirtier than Frippo's.

The first time we met, Jacques said, "This is *Ay liz a bet a."*

"Ah, oui," said Bawdy. "Eh. English? American? You're American?"

I nodded. "French is better than English!" he spat at me. "Don't you think France is better than America? Yes, French is much better than English." He stomped his foot in emphasis. I was too shocked to think of a witty comeback. *No, France sucks!* Or, *America is much better, you fool!*

"I am here," I said, demure, pleased to evade the question. That's how I was raised, of course. Avoid conflict. Be polite. To make it worse, Michel chimed in "*La Belle Amérique*," in a snide voice.

What? Michel hates Americans, too? Do the Fontaines hate Americans, all Americans except, perhaps, me? The family seems to appreciate that I am willing to work hard, and that I make the effort to try. They don't write me off, like they do the rest of America. That's my guess, anyway.

Why, if the French hate America so much, do they play old French songs about New York and California on the radio all day? The fact that English replaced French as the international language irritated the hell out of Bawdy. Periodically, the radio spews news like, "Eight million unemployed in America" and "Children in America spend more time watching TV than in school"—all bad news. Since I arrived in France, I've said, "I'm American" more times than ever in my life. The French seem both attracted and repelled. I want to feel proud of being an American, but in reality, I am ambivalent. Some parts of the United States I love. Some, I don't.

This rainy Thursday evening Bawdy roars, spouting words I don't understand, yammering on and on. Camilla ignores him as she stirs the fire underneath the cauldron. The Fontaines might not like Bawdy, but they tolerate him because he's their only neighbor, and he possesses something absolutely precious to the children: a television. When Marie and Louis finish their supper, they leap off the benches and scamper across the street to watch TV, their weekly routine.

Once the children leave with Bawdy, I wash the dishes while Camilla dries. "Would you like to make an apple cake?"

"Ah, oui." I like cooking, but keeping the wood just right for the correct temperature in the stove is tough. I start peeling an apple, trying to flick my wrist like Marian. I imagine her thin, bony wrist, and that twist she does, one twirl, and magically, the full apple is peeled and a single peel remains for the rabbits to nibble. I have seven apples to

peel. Usually, I end up with two or three peels. With each apple, I cut longer and longer swirls from my knife. Finally, there's only one, long, curly peel. Marian, you taught me well.

"*Ay liz a bet a,*" Camilla surprises me with a fifty-note franc. "Here's your monthly pay." Or, at least that's what I assume she says as she hands me the note, the equivalent of about ten dollars.

"*Merci,*" I say. I didn't know what I'd get paid. It looks like my wage is ten dollars a month, working six days a week, with every Wednesday off. Oh well, it's cheaper than going to the gym to get strong, or to Outward Bound, or some health spa in Arizona.

"How long are you planning to stay?"

You'd have thought we'd have worked this out a while ago, but we hadn't. I weigh the pros and cons of staying through the winter. I'm so serene on the hills, tending the goats, meditating, writing in my journal. Mostly, the puzzles inspire me—understanding people's French, figuring out how to work more efficiently, exploring the hillside on my days off. My self-doubt is shedding, peeling away layers of feeling "less than." I love being so close to nature, feeling like I'm living my true spiritual life.

And there's Randy. The other day when he came in from herding, his hair tussled by the wind, he looked more like a man than the young boy he seemed at first. I find myself oddly attracted to him. That may not be a good thing. We're like a secret club, speaking our own language, getting closer and closer.

The weather's changing, though. Before my cousin returned to America, he warned me about the savage mountain winters, brutal with snow, wind, and freezing rain. The winds are so powerful, he said, they each carry their own name: *Tramontane, Le Vent Cers, Le Vent Sirocco* and *Le Vent Autan.* But that's the challenge I want to face: to stick out the winter, survive the hard times. To be a true goatherd, I need to herd in the worst of times, not just the best.

When I first accepted this job, I wasn't sure what I wanted. Now my goal is clear. I want to learn to believe in myself. How can I do that if I quit before the hard times?

I hear my Mom's voice in my ears. If I'm going to do this, I'm going to do it right, which means herd through the winter, no matter how harsh it is. "I'll work until spring," I say to Camilla. "I'll herd through the winter and leave in March."

Camilla nods, than speaks quietly, nearly a whisper. "*Randy*," she says, "*est très, très timide, n'est ce pas*?" Randy is very, very timid, isn't he? Her black eyes pin me, dark, like a well deep in the earth.

"Yes." *Oui,* very timid. *Oui,* precious and vulnerable. Every time Marian and Jean visit, Randy withdraws into his shell. Since he and I are so close, I forget how other people scare him, how he almost hides from strangers. Maybe Camilla is really saying, be careful of his tender feelings.

With the children at Bawdy's, the only sounds are sticks sizzling in the fire. Camilla embroiders; Randy sketches with charcoal; and Jacques peruses a book on the Native

American cultures of the Apache and Sioux that he'd like to emulate here in Languedoc. I park myself on the hearth, warmed by fire and write in my journal.

I'm well-suited to being a goatherd, to tending my goats and sheep and cow, and to spending evenings in virtual silence when everyone works on his or her own project. My mom used to tell me how content I was at age three and four visiting my grandmother, humming to myself, building castles and garages and cities out of stacks of cottage-cheese containers.

Mom brought groceries every week to my grandmother's second-floor apartment in the old Victorian house. I remember antiques and Oriental rugs and the scent of Chanel No. 5. My mom chatted with my grandmother in her cheery red and yellow kitchen, the aroma of chocolate-chip cookies fresh and delicious. I played on the rug happily by myself. I'd hum and eat my cookies, never interrupting.

What my Mother didn't know, what no one knew, was that my eardrums were blocked. I talked "funny" because I couldn't hear. I was the only one who could understand the deaf man who parked the cars for the department store. By the time my tonsils and adenoids were removed at age four, I'd learned to talk "wrong." Even with speech therapy at school and elocution lessons on Saturday, people thought I talked "funny."

Through junior high and high school, I left speech classes behind, believing the problem had disappeared, and was surprised when my debate teacher at Ohio Wesleyan suggested I test with a speech therapist.

My heart pattered rapidly when I met with the speech therapist to receive my test results. My hands gripped the chair, sweaty even in the Ohio winter, as my eyes skated over her diplomas while she read the report.

She leaned forward; I leaned back. My stomach lurched, afraid of her next words.

"Since you don't speak correctly," she began, "People need to work hard to understand your words and what you're saying. It takes work to hear you, work to listen." I smelled the chrysanthemums on her desk. "And often, people just give up. They don't bother to listen."

"Do you feel like people just write you off?" she asked me. A tear dribbled down my cheek. "The reason it feels like people aren't listening to you is, they aren't."

The click of the clock sounded like a hammer pounding. I remained still for a moment, dazed, and quietly rose, shutting the door behind me. The streetlight shone on the cracks in the sidewalk, and light snowflakes shimmered, dancing in its beam. *If people never listen to me, no wonder I don't believe in myself.* I began to sob.

Now in the *salle à manger,* Marie and Louis rush into the house, home from Bawdy's. They fling their sopping wet coats over the chairs and wring out their hair by the fire, babbling faster than I can follow, excited about their movie, or TV show, I don't know which. Circling the table, high on sugar, they finally settle with books and papers and pencils.

"Ay liz a bet a," Marie says, "Will you help me with my English homework?" It's the only time she's asked, so I'm eager to help.

"Sure." I leaf through her textbook, reading a caption, "America," under a photo of a decrepit tenement with bricks disintegrating into dust, smashed glass smattered over ripped cement, trash mingled with weeds—a scene from the Bronx, unsafe to walk on a Sunday morning. Yes, that's America. One version.

"For my English homework," Marie says, "I need to write what this means: what's 'another brick in the wall?'"

"What's 'another brick in the wall?!'" I laugh, wondering about the teacher who assigned Pink Floyd for English class. I've sung the song a hundred times, but I've never really thought about the meaning. "Well, it's like we're all the same. Like we don't have any individuality." I ponder. "But what it really means is: if we don't watch out, we'll become all the same. In fact, we're truly unique, each and every one of us. But we tend to forget that, and fuse together with everyone else. We need to watch out, or we will be a brick in the wall."

My French is too spotty to convey all I mean, but Marie nods her head slowly, her mouth a small curve, as though she understands what I'm trying to say. "What are your other assignments?" I ask.

She hands me her notebook with her scrawls in black ink. "I'm learning how a faucet works—see here?" She points to her sketch. "And we're drawing plans for a house." She flips through a few pages. "And how to make a cassette box."

"Wow," I say, impressed. Well, I learned French, Latin, English, and math at MacDuffie School for Girls. That's about it. When I transferred, and boarded at Northfield

Mount Hermon, we had a class that met in a cabin by the pond that counted for English, history, and religion credit. That was cool.

"You know," I say, "there are so many things that are similar but different in France and America. For instance, Americans always have cotton in our pill bottles, instead of foam, like you do. And your aspirin always has vitamin C in it. I've never seen that before."

"C'est vrai?" asks Marie.

"Yeah, really. And when we write letters to mail, we write the first name, followed by the last name, opposite from the way you write them."

Marie laughs.

I head to bed, but before I say good night, I notice Michel, quiet at the edge of the table. He's been sitting there all evening, nursing his wine. I've never seen him so sad, like his world fell out from under him. *"À toute à l'heure* I say, with a slight wave, wishing I could converse with him.

The next morning, I wake shivering. I layer my clothes: long underwear, turtleneck, sweaters, and Jacques' old, ripped, brown leather coat. When I leave the house, I blow frosty vapor rings.

So, this is the cold Elton warned about. My eyes water in the icy air, under the dull, grey sky. In the refrigerator-like barn, sheep mesh together against the wall, their ears back, and my Baby hides in a corner against a bale of hay. No one wants to leave the barn in this frigid weather.

"*Allez*," I call. "Come on, guys." We hike over the first hill, and the clouds darken, peeling freezing rain from the sky. Fog surrounds us, and thunder pounds like dropping bombs.

With my mittened hands, I bend down a high branch for Baby and Elusive to reach. I think back on last night, when I helped Marie with her homework, and Michel sat slumped with his eyes damp, red, in a pool of sorrow. A broken relationship? A heartbreak? Our entwined family group absorbs each other's moods, feelings, and thoughts as though by osmosis. Now, out here on the mountain, I remember Michel's grief, and cry in empathy. Emotions feel raw and open living so close to nature—every feeling, up front and present. It's like being on my period 24/7.

That's what it's like being here in the hills, surrounded by Nature. Only Nature. The sounds and sights and smells all heighten, and a sixth sense, a psychic sense, vibrates. Just like Camilla and Marie, my period starts with each full moon. I dream constantly and vividly. One night I write in my journal, *I dreamed I had a baby named Kristen,* which shocks me thirty years later when I review my 1980 journal to write this very book. In fact my husband, Paul, chose the name 'Kristen' for my only child, born fifteen years after my journal entry.

At the Fontaines, I feel receptive, intuitive, unlike ever before. Family lore says my prim Bostonian great-grandmother used to read the newspaper in her parlor, the scent of jasmine drifting through the open window. The neighbor often visited to discuss the children, the garden, and oh, by the way, the horse races. Months later, my great-grandmother was shocked to discover the neighbor was betting—and winning—on the horses based on my great-grandmother's psychic knowledge. Immediately, her gift of predicting the winners disappeared.

Jacques never carries a watch, yet arrives for dinner promptly at noon, whether the sun is out or behind the rain clouds. He forecasts weather, and plants his crops according to the moon. Soon enough, I, too, begin to "know" time and can herd without a watch.

Call it intuition, call it psychic power, call it the Irish fey, it's fundamental to life here at this remote farm.

The rain spills from the sky as my goats and I rush to the barn, already soaked. Before I can hang up my drenched coat, Randy says, "You have a package."

"My first package! But it's all ripped up? God, someone tore through the brown paper and pried into the box! What happened? This is in shreds! "

"Apparently," Randy says, "the *gendarmes*—the police—inspect every package."

"What? They rip open *every* package?" I remove the dangling string which once held my mom's careful packing. "They think we're getting drugs or something?"

Camilla hustles into the kitchen, pushes her glasses up her nose, and asks, "What do you have?" We're all thrilled to see a package. I rip off the rest of the paper, and lift the lid. "Oh," cries Camilla. *"C'est beau!"* I hold up a light-blue, Gortex, L.L. Bean jacket with a plaid flannel lining.

"C'est beau indeed!" Randy and I now speak our own little mixture of French and English. "And look, more!" Underneath the coat is a matching blue plaid wool shirt. "And black leather gloves! These are beautiful. And more

long underwear." I hold them up. "This is what I really need!"

"There's more," Camilla says, pointing.

Oh, books! "Randy, check these out. All the classics I wish I'd read in school—Austin, Eliot, Tolstoy, and more," I say.

"Good," he says. "We were running low."

"For someone who never read much before, you sure are making up for lost time."

He knows it's true. Our mothers are sending us loads of books. He's become an avid reader, and I'm learning all about Australia. Handy to know how to survive in the fiery deserts of Australia while I'm shivering in the freezing mountains of France.

Ferocious winds chill my bones that afternoon on the hills. "Stop, Georgia," I say, after she knocks Elusive to the side. "Quit that. Come here, Elusive," I call. Of course, she won't. Elusive is still like a cat eyeing me from a distance. I shake a branch so nuts fall, and I stuff my pockets full. Baby bounces over—she never strays too far from me—and Chinny and Harrison trot to eat the goodies in my hand. I pretend I'm not paying attention, and catch Elusive sneaking closer. I turn quickly, and she dashes away, lithe on her thin stick legs. "I'm just kidding," I say to Elusive. "Just go eat from the tree. I won't bother you."

When my mind's not occupied, the default setting is Garner. I remember an old friend saying, "I'm going to guard my heart. I'm not going to let myself fall for anyone." Why did I even fall for Garner? Something about him seemed so sharp, so bright, so exciting. Was that why? Was I attracted because he grew up dirt poor, with nothing, and didn't judge me at all?

He seemed unfettered by any social mores. Not chained to propriety, to rules of etiquette. So, why did this attract me? Maybe because I always felt judged—by the college I chose, by my appearance, by a general sense of ineptness. I judged other people—that was engrained in my upbringing. And yet, I failed by those very standards. With Garner, my feeling of failure evaporated.

Garner was a lost soul himself. Not healthy for me. I wanted to change him. Oh, I wish I had someone to talk to about Garner—a girlfriend here in France who could give me advice, who could tell me what to do. Marian would be perfect. With her head high and her air of confidence, she seems so wise, sure of herself. And yet, between my *mauvais* French and Marian's zero English, we still can't carry on a conversation.

"*Allez*," I call. Jam, a big, old goat saunters around the bend. "Come on back." Yes, Marian and I have a language barrier, but even so, she seems to wall away her spirit. She's so mysterious. I remember in junior high how I'd fixate on girls I wanted to emulate. That's what it's like with Marian. I'd love to be her friend.

Marian has a stronger accent than most, which adds to our communication problems. Centuries ago, the people of this area spoke their own language, *Langue d'Oc*. Since we're a long way from Paris, the residents of Languedoc still speak with a heavy accent, adding an "a" at the end of every word, so that "*Aylizabet*" in Paris becomes "*Ay liz a bet a*" here.

How would you advise me, Marian, if you understood my dilemma? Would you say I should have stayed and tried to work it out with Garner? Or, would you say I made the right decision to come here? Here, I'll come to know life on life's terms. Here, I'll shed the feeling of being "less than." Here, I'll learn to believe in myself.

Baby squirms, orbiting me, his little ribs rubbing against my calves. When he nuzzles his cold nose against me, I lift him to my chest and hug him tightly. The winds thrash us, and I yearn to be back at the house, warming myself in front of the yellow-spitting, ragged flames.

My throat constricts. So often, my emotions spike and crash unpredictably. Today, my longing for Garner overpowers me. I plod home with my herd, my head down, lonely, cold, depressed. Back at the barn, I rope the goats and sheep and Ma Rosa in their stalls, and after the last partition is tied, Michel and Marie surprise me. They've never met me in the barn before, except to milk the goats.

"*Bienvenu,*" they say. "Welcome home!" Their smiles shine so gaily, with such comfort. Marie clasps her arm around me, the closest I've gotten to a hug since my arrival here. Michel kisses me on each cheek twice, and grins. Did they pick up on my lonely feelings? How did they know how depressed I felt? But that's how it is here. We soak up one another's feelings like a paper towel sops up milk. Their greeting warms me, and together we *promenade* back to the house.

Chapter Five

Ma Rosa

Grey clouds circle overhead the next morning, and a light drizzle trickles from the sky. "*Allez*," I call to my herd, coaxing them out of the barn. First, Ma Rosa bats her long, black lashes. She moseys along our herding trail, and swishes her tail, jerking her head back and forth to swat the flies, and stops. Halts. Does not flinch. Does not move her legs. Does not twitch a muscle. "*Allez. Allez.* Get going, Ma Rosa." The stubborn cow (perhaps as stubborn as that part of me who still clings to Garner) doesn't budge. I holler again and a third time. The scent of mud mixes with thyme. Ma Rosa, the dame who forgets she is actually a cow, towers over me, staring ahead with her marsh-brown eyes. The goats skip ahead and disappear over the hillside. I faintly hear their bells. "*Ma Rosa!*" I scream again and again until my throat is raw.

"Frippo," I finally say, wiping the rain from my face and tightening my wool scarf around my neck. "Go on, Frippo." No matter if I speak in French or English, Frippo understands. He and Natasha are my buddies—mangy, loyal, friends, and even though Randy shuns them both because they bite the goats, I rely on them for times like this.

Frippo and Natasha cock their heads, jump, and chew at Ma Rosa's heel until at last she slogs along. She creeps five steps, and abruptly stops again. The winds whistle through the shrubs as I swat her massive body, her prickly hide. For minutes we freeze in a standoff. I take a deep breath, ready to holler. Finally, like a scene in a slow-motion movie, she bends her knee, lifts her leg off the ground, holds it for one, five, ten seconds, and suddenly, POW! She drops her enormous hoof hard and fast right on my big toe. All her million pounds, smack! Bull's eye!

My scream can be heard over hills and valleys around the world. "OWWW!"

She must weigh 350 pounds. "Ma Rosa!" I cry. She doesn't move. She doesn't glance at me. Statue-still, like an obstinate teenager, she ignores me, twirls her tail, and chomps on her disgusting cud. I feel my toe swelling underneath her massive weight. Ohh, I despise that Ma Rosa!

I might not mind so much if the rest of the family hated her, too. But noooo, they looove their "sweet" Ma Rosa. For what feels like hours, she flattens my toe like a lemon crepe. "Ma Rosa!" Rain mixes with my tears, and finally, that awful, awful cow deigns to lift her foot and lumber on, up the trail.

"Ow!" I shriek again. With my foot now free, my big toe first feels numb, and aches with a searing pain. I limp behind Ma Rosa with my fists clenched so tightly that my nails draw blood. At the top of the hill, Baby and Elusive and the gang munch leaves while the sheep graze on yellow grass. The pain in my toe grows, my head throbs, and the goats' bells sound like a child banging a pot with a wooden spoon. Ma Rosa stands regally, indifferent, aloof, in a world her own.

I untie my super cool, totally worthless, New Balance sneakers. The glue that adheres the soles to the body of the sneaker has worn off from all the trudging in the mud. I tear off my socks, now wet and sticking to my foot, and watch my toe morph: pale blue becomes purple as it swells to the size of a golf ball. There's no way it will fit back in my shoe. My toe, my otherwise unappreciated toe, looks like an LA sunset. And oh, how it burns.

The following day, Randy leads our goats and sheep and ornery Ma Rosa, whom I hate, hate, hate, into the chafing winds. I limp behind with Baby. What a rare treat to herd with Randy. The goats circle him like he is St. Francis of Assisi reincarnated, who, perhaps, he is. I unstrap my backpack, spilling my books and tape player onto a nearby rock. "Randy," I ask. "What do you miss the most about home?"

"Mmm. He glances to the side, rubbing Minor's spotted head. "I don't know." This small boy-man speaks, barely moving his lips, like the Queen of England, who is said to eat without opening her mouth. "I guess I miss my Mum most."

"Anything else?"

Randy flaps Chinny's long, soft ears, draping her face like a dangling mop. "Not ri-lly," he says, in that lovely Australian accent.

"You know what I miss? I miss soooo much? Baths. Warm, bubbly baths." I veer away from the wind that scratches my face like steel wool. At home, baths used to be my solace, my reward at the end of each day. I'd light candles set on the rim of the tub, across the sink, even on the floor—and turn on the new age music, like a harp, or cello. I'd pour drops of Calgon Bath Oil into the scalding water, scenting the room like sweet perfume. When the water had cooled just a smidgen, I dipped one toe, then the next, and at last my whole body, until I floated in the warm, silky water, candles flickering around me, heaven on earth.

Oh, how I miss my baths. My therapy. Every night here on the farm, baths take over my dreams. Somehow, sitting on a hard chair in the stone kitchen, wiping my body with a rag in lukewarm water, my feet sunk in a dish pan, doesn't cut it for me.

I also miss my family and friends. And milkshakes. And parties. But every night, I dream of baths.

Time to move to the next spot. *"Allez,"* Randy and I both call. *"Allez."* The bells tinkle as the herd draws closer, and darts ahead toward the next grove of trees. Baby skims my calves, skipping along, while Elusive hangs back. We stride past an open pasture where Jacques' pride and joy, three Camargue horses, graze near the temporary fence which Jacques moves from time to time.

Jacques loves these giant, grey horses with rectangular, box-shaped noses, enormous eyes, broad ears, and short, muscular necks. They nod their heads, acknowledging us, and return to chewing their grasses and herbs. The Camargues are Jacques' greatest passion. I can't pinpoint why, but I begin to feel a sense of grace emanating from the horses, as though they exude a sacred feeling of the divine, solid and profound.

The sun springs through a swarm of clouds, and a rainbow forms. Three goats start jousting. Georgia and Jam leap with their legs up, and Split-Infinitive plants herself in the middle. They coo and grunt and, watching them fight bothers me at first, but they're like kids, wrestling on the playground. When they butt a bit too rough, Randy waves his hands. "Shoo! Shoo!" he yells. And they do.

I survey our herd—the sheep tightly nestled, pregnant Ma Rosa chewing grass, and the goats munching on the trees. A small goat, Minor, lies off to the side, away from the others. He's still, unmoving. The wind furls my coat as I jog over to him for a better view. He's as motionless as the rocks around him. "Randy! Come here! Quick!"

Randy holds his hand in front of Minor's mouth to see if he's breathing, and rests his hands on Minor's stomach and head. "Minor's dead." His voice is slow, solemn.

"Dead? He can't be dead. Can he? How?"

Randy gazes out at the miles of open fields, strewn with boulders. "I don't know." The boy's eyes drop, his cheeks cave, his mouth tightens. He lifts Minor carefully, wrapping the back and front hooves around his neck and walks back to the barn. Through the howl of the wind and softly ringing goats' bells, the world feels suddenly hushed.

There could have been a number of reasons why Minor died, but I didn't know that then. A deep gash could lead to tetanus. We should have trimmed the goats' hooves every six weeks to prevent hoof rot. We should have dusted everyone for mites and parasites on a regular basis to help our goats stay healthy, to help more babies survive later on. We shouldn't have been out in these storms.

I lift Baby onto my lap, and pet her short hair. I feel a hole in my stomach. I've lost an acquaintance, not really a friend. My chest tightens. It's hard to breathe. Accepting death is part of a farmer's life. For me, it's just beginning.

At the end of the afternoon, pouring rains drench us once more, and at supper, no one speaks. I can't eat, thinking of Minor, so still, silent. The radio broadcasts news of the election, but I catch only a few words: America, Jimmy Carter, Ronald Reagan, The White House.

I fall asleep to the rain and wake up with more rain. I lived in Oregon for six years, so daily rain is not unusual. But here, working outdoors every day, is different. Up on the soggy hills, I open my hand of nuts for Harrison and Baby, but Lucy barges between us to get the goodies first. I imagine Minor, his body so still, inert, and try to shake off his image by singing in my horribly off-key voice, screwing up the lyrics. *"Give me a ticket for an airplane!"* I bellow. This is my survival—singing and dancing in the rain. I sing, picturing Garner writing to me, asking me to marry him. Ah, the illusions of first love.

On Saturday, with no school and no place to be, Marie and Louis chase each other around the table, screaming and hitting, so obnoxious that I want to holler, "Stop! Shut up! You're driving me crazy!" Noon dinner feels like no break at all. Camilla and Marie yell at each other until Marie clomps out, crying. Between this vile weather, missing Garner, and the screaming kids, my nerves fray. Camilla serves the goat stew, fragrant with red wine. We're all exhausted, and the only sounds are chewing and *Louisianne.*

Part of me feels like leaving, but I've made my commitment. Besides, what would I do? I did way too many drugs in Oregon, and it occurs to me that my openness and clarity here on the mountain might be because I'm drug-free for the first time in years. I don't want to go back to the same life I left behind. It's not like I'd suddenly write my book, although both my mom and grandmother have asked. No, my life would be just as aimless as it was when I cocktail waitressed. I'll stay here and finish this somewhat ambiguous mission.

Randy washes the dishes after dinner, while I dry. "Why do you think everyone's arguing?" I ask him.

"I don't have a clue."

After noon dinner, Randy makes *fromage de chèvre,* and I herd in the soupy mud which seeps into my shoes. As we round a bend, we pass a crumbling stone hut which once provided rest for shepherds in decades or centuries past. I'll come back and explore it someday.

I want to accomplish great things—someday, somehow. I mull possibilities. During college in Oregon, I worked long hours at White Bird, the free crisis clinic. The simplest path for me would be to get a Masters in Social Work. But, if that is the course of least resistance, does it represent the easy way out? Social work comes naturally to me. But is there something harder, more in line with my true passions? Like writing?

When I consider my desire to write, I imagine the Ansel Adams photograph with boulders leading up to the clouded mountain. It's elusive—like Garner, like Elusive, it never gets closer. And yet writing calls to me, and feels as inscribed into my DNA as clearly as my eye color.

In second grade, I wrote my first play in my enormous bedroom closet sitting in my tiny black-armed chair at my family's antique, child-sized roll-top desk. My play, "Lillie and Millie Go to Mars," starred me, my best friend Amy, and our turtles. We planned to perform in our garage, but it snowed so hard the day of the show, we canceled.

A few weeks later, I saw *The Wizard of Oz*. Oh, no, my seven year old self thought. Dorothy's house flew to Oz by the power of a tornado! That's what I wrote in my play—the children and their turtles flew to Mars by a tornado. My idea must not be original! I must have known about the tornado in *The Wizard of Oz*, and forgotten about it. If I'm not original, I can't be a writer! *There's no point in ever writing again.* And so ended my writing career. Or, at least, delayed it for decades.

How easily I shut down myself, I think in retrospect. Shut down my dreams, my passion, my belief in myself. Out here on the hills, I am resurrecting a part of myself, and in a sense rebirthing myself. Just because the *Wizard of Oz* had a tornado, doesn't mean I can never write again. It doesn't mean I need to waste my life. It doesn't mean I'm an unworthy person. My little girl's brain tried to reason so well, and yet was so wrong.

Coconut ambles around the hillside, out of sight. "Damn it, Coconut! *Allez, allez!*" I knit my eyebrows, annoyed. "Okay Frippo, go get Coconut. But don't bite her!" My scruffy companion barks, bouncing up at my "*allez,*" and leaps in the direction of my pointed finger, his scraggy tail flopping from side to side. Coconut's bells clang from over the hillside and moments later, she rushes to me with Frippo at her ankles. "Enough! Frippo, back off!" Coconut joins her buddies, and Frippo lies down, resuming his doggy dreams of chasing goats and sheep with no human holding him back.

Back at the house, Michel, Jacques, Jean, and other friends I don't know crack jokes in the *salle à manger* with their empty wine bottles strewn across the table. "What's going on?" I ask Randy, as I rip off my soaking wet hat that clings to my damp hair, stringy like French-cut beans.

Randy shrugs. "They're talking about bringing the horses down from the mountains?" Roars of laughter bellow from the other room.

"What does Michel say?" I ask.

"I haven't a clue." Such is our ongoing confusion. Which horses do they bring from the mountain? Where do they take them? Whose horses are they? Whatever, the men are having a good ole time. Jacques is a changed man with bottles of wine. The quiet soul chuckles, yaks, and jokes with his friends, but he doesn't become obnoxious. I just wish I knew what they were celebrating.

After dinner, when Michel, Jean, and the other boys leave, Jacques shows me his finished project: a leather strap of bells that he's been crafting for weeks. He jingles them, just when the telephone rings. "*Ay liz a bet a!*" Marie calls. "Telephone!" Marie hands me one earpiece of the old black rotary which has a second earpiece attached with a cord, like I've never seen. Marie puts the second earpiece to her ear so she can to listen in on the conversation, giggling in her excitement —a call from *Amérique!* The fact that she doesn't understand a word of our English conversation doesn't deter her one iota from eavesdropping.

My mom is on one phone, with my dad on the extension. I stretch the phone cord around my fingers, thrilled to hear their voices because from ten thousand miles away, my parents seem far less flawed. "Herding is going well. Baby follows me everywhere," I say. "Elusive still won't let me touch her. We're not getting as much milk, so cheese-making is pretty slow."

"What would you like me to send?" my mom asks. I stare at dust particles dancing near the tiny window. An oil furnace to warm the house? A hot, snuggly bubble bath?

"It's pretty cold." I say. "Just what you sent before would be great. More long underwear. Even more books. Randy and I share them. Oh, and could you send some French vocab cards? My French is getting better, but it has a long way to go." I sigh. In all my years of summer camp, boarding school, college in Ohio and Oregon, I've never missed my family like I do living here. Yet, I'm convinced this is where I need be.

Wednesday is my one day off for the week. After breakfast, I hike to the top of the hill across the street. A wooden cross twice my height stands among piles of boulders, perhaps ruins of a chapel. For the first time in my life, I enjoy hiking and climbing. I'm actually liking exercise. My arms are getting strong, my legs are stronger, and my body's more flexible. I think of my mom's belief that the panacea for all ills is fresh air and exercise. That may be true!

I inhale the wild sage, and view our *petit* village of only four houses, surrounded by miles of rocky hills. This cross, which can be seen for miles in all directions, might have memorialized events of World War I. Or maybe World War II? Or was it ancient, from the time of the gory Crusades?

My cousin, Elton, explained to me that the people from Languedoc, now and in the past, have always been independent. "Since the people of Languedoc lived so far from Paris, they maintained their autonomy for years. About a thousand years ago, many people in Languedoc practiced their own form of Christianity, Catherism, rather than strict Catholicism. The Cathers might have been left alone with their odd beliefs, if it weren't for one stickler. The Cathers didn't believe in tithing to the Pope."

Natasha bounds up the hillside, and curls in a ball next to me. I pet her head, remembering my history conversation with Elton.

"The Pope staged the first crusade of Christians against Christians," Elton had said. "The story goes that when the general asked the Pope, 'How do we know who's a Catholic and who's a Cather?' The response was, 'Kill them all! Let God sort them out.' The result was genocide, and twenty thousand people, nearly the entire population of Beziers, the city on the Mediterranean were murdered."

"Did any Cathers live?" I'd asked.

"There are lots of stories, myths, that some survived, hiding in the mountains where they continue to live, keeping their religion in private."

The next morning I awake with mattress lumps jabbing into my back and frigid winds seeping through the rafters. It's as cold as the Bering Straits. I'm exhausted after yet another night with little sleep. Marie wrestled the blankets off me during the night. I yanked them back, and she rolled over again, swiping them all. Some days are better than others.

Camilla greets me in the kitchen with *"Bonjour,"* and a radiant smile. *Shut up,* I think, wanting to bury my head and hide from her cheer. I yawn, and pour a cup of my hot chicory-coffee. Broadcasters shout news about the American presidential election on the radio.

I favor Carter, who stands up for the little guy and the environment. Reagan champions the "trickle down" theory of economics. With his plan, taxes will be cut for the rich. "Money will trickle down to the poor," he claims. Ha! I don't believe it for a minute.

Camilla strolls into the *salle à manger,* wiping her hands on her apron. "Randy will herd this morning and I've got mending for you." I nod and sip another spoonful of my breakfast milk.

A half hour later, I edge my bench to the fire and sort through the pile of shirts, pants, and coats. With Marie's blue blouse in hand, I comb through the buttons in Camilla's straw sewing box until I find a white pearl button that matches Marie's blouse. "Ow!" The needle spears into my finger as I sew on buttons, patch holes in Jacques' grey pants, and mend rips in Camilla's blouses. I tilt my work toward the dim silver rays that siphon through the window.

Camilla bounds over to examine a blouse. "This button isn't straight," she says in a cross voice. "This thread is the wrong color." She returns again and again to inspect my work. "These stitches aren't even." The fire smells of green wood, smoky pine. I imagine I'm seeing myself from afar, a young woman hunkered over her sewing before a fire in the cold, stone house. "These stitches are too big." Camilla says, frowning. "You should use a smaller needle. Is that all you've finished? You need to sew more quickly."

My stomach churns, stirring with lumps of emotion. I'm a failure, says the old tape in my brain. Incompetent, once again. I pull myself out of these sunken emotions, haul myself from self-loathing. But then, I judge myself more. If I had more faith in myself, I think as a log thuds in the fireplace, I wouldn't let Camilla get to me. But she does get to me, and when I sleep poorly, like last night, all my defenses fall away. I'm not going to cry, I tell myself.

But when Camilla returns to the kitchen to stir the goat's milk for cheese, I think, wait a minute. I haven't felt this way—beating myself up—in a long time. I used to feel like shit all the time. Worthless, a weakling, less than. Now, I rarely sink so low. Camilla criticizes me a lot, sure, but I've improved. I don't get down on myself so much. More often than not, I think, oh, shit! I've screwed up, but I'll get it sooner or later. I should credit myself for my growth. I'm so much kinder to myself than I used to be. And that *is* growth.

"Humph!" I may have said aloud. I look around, laugh at myself, seeing no one is in the room. I'm not perfect, but I'm beginning to accept my humanness, which doesn't mean I am the smartest, the hardest worker, or the cleverest, but whoever I am, my heart, my soul, and my inner flame are sincere and compassionate. I repeat an old mantra. "Compassion is the wisdom. Wisdom is the compassion." I feel smothered under this pile of mending, so I'm having a setback, succumbing to Camilla's criticism. And I am really, really tired.

In the afternoon, I call to the goats, many of whom have vanished in the damp, silver mist. I'm reading *Lost Horizons,* the story of a member of the British diplomatic corps who lands in Utopia, a monastery hidden deep in the mountains of Tibet. He finds peace, love, and a sense of purpose. A perfect book for me here in France, where I pray and mediate and dwell on spirituality.

Oddly, my daily rituals—reading spiritual literature, praying, and meditating—all started as part of my path to lose weight. Back when my mom was released from the

ICU, still sick, but alive, I wanted to leave MacDuffie School for Girls, where perfectly sculpted, two-foot ice sculptures at lunch were the norm. I applied and was accepted at Northfield Mount Hermon, where I'd live in dorms junior and senior year.

Being overweight obsessed me in middle school and high school. I weighed myself every day, counted every calorie, and in tenth grade, begged my parents to send me to Camp Stanley, a "fat girl's camp" in the Adirondack Mountains that I'd found advertised in the back of the *New York Times* magazine. Reluctantly, they agreed to the ridiculously expensive camp. My bunk mates and I spent all summer complaining about the camp, about the director, and about the food. We were weighed every week, exercised, kept track of our measurements, and took classes in makeup and clothes.

Here was the strange part. Even though we came from all over the country, we felt like kin, like sisters, like for once someone understood us. Understood what it felt like to be embarrassed by our bodies, to feel shame and doubt and self-hatred. To be the "good friend who listens." We'd dieted; we'd vomited; we'd starved. We'd lost weight and gained weight, and here at Camp Stanley, we connected like no other friends before.

In fall, after "fat girl's camp," I started at Northfield. My biology partner was Sidney Poitier's daughter, and I ate lunch with Eunice and Maria Shriver when they toured the campus. But I created my own lonely, miserable hell, stealing ten muffins at a time from the dorm kitchen, eating cherry pie from the garbage, and sinking deeper and deeper into depression. Desperately lonely, I slept constantly, barely passing my classes. I gained sixty pounds, 130 to 190, from September to January.

Then, stranger than strange, I was chosen to be a prefect for the freshman dorm. Out of two hundred girls in my class, the faculty selected me to be one of the four seniors in charge of the freshmen, to guide them, to offer support. Me, the obese, acne-faced, friendless girl; I was the one they thought would be a great leader.

When someone believes in you, it's easier to believe in yourself. What did they see in me, these faculty? That I was, perhaps, kind and caring, responsible and honest, someone who could be counted on in an emergency? All true. I started to take care of myself, walking two miles before class, eating salads, and ending my food binges.

As a senior in a freshman dorm filled with fourteen-year-olds, I felt comfortable. We knit and played bridge in our old brick dormitory with its thick oak woodwork and musk-smelling Oriental rugs. Still, I had no dates, no boyfriends, attended no parties.

My weight still yo-yoed, and after my stint of college in Ohio, I moved to Oregon. "I'm perfectly happy," I said to my therapist. "But look at me. I'm sixty pounds overweight. Something must be wrong." Between counseling and meditation and spiritual programs for overeaters, I eventually, over several years, lost my extra weight. That's when Garner came along.

Why did I fall for him? Was it because it's easier to go from a fat body to a thin body than to go from a fat mind to a thin mind? Is that why people gain all their weight back?

On the one hand, we who lose weight still hold the shame, the doubt, the lack of confidence that mired us down when we were fat. I, like most women, started dressing super sexy after losing weight. Do we believe that because we were 'too fat to be sexy' before, now we have to overcompensate? We throw out our old "fat wardrobe" and buy a new sexy wardrobe. And, of course, men appear like vultures, and we haven't learned how to defend ourselves from them except by being fat, so we gain back all our weight. And the result is, we believe in ourselves less than ever. For me, growing a "thin mind," recognizing my worth, learning to believe in myself, was my mission here in the mountains of Languedoc.

"*Ay liz a bet a.*" Jacques startles me, appearing beyond the veil of fog like in a scene from a Humphrey Bogart movie. "Three goats were eating the leeks in the garden," he says, his nostrils flared. Shit. So much for the mist's illusion of privacy. So much for my superb goat tending. I glance at the mischievous trio, Georgia, Split-Infinitive, and Baby, who wander to the leaves of the nearly barren trees. I glance at my feet and wiggle my toes. Busted. "True goatherds," Jacques once told me, "don't read or write in their journal or practice their French. They're just there with the goats." Well, I guess I'm not a true goatherd. Not yet, anyway.

"*Allez,*" I call, in case other goats have strayed beyond the wall of fog. Jacques disappears in silence. My heart heaves, and slowly tears trickle down my cheeks. I've cried with my goats; I've laughed; I've sung; I've danced. Herding under this endless sky, in miles of nature, miles of blue mountains, I feel like the whole world and I are connected, a giant umbilical cord tying us all together.

That evening at dinner, a Parisian commentator in New York once again discusses the November Presidential election, just a few days away. "The American political parties are all the same," Jacques says. "Democrats and Republicans—they're all the same. Like having just one party. They're all rich."

"I don't care who the American President is," Randy scoffs. "You know, we in Australia live as well as you do in America without all your wars." Camilla cares too little about the elections to comment.

I think Reagan is an idiot. God, I wish I understood what the commentators jabber about for hours on end. It turns out that Carter urged Reagan to debate. Disaster. Reagan, a brilliant actor, said to the American public during the debate, *"Ask yourself, are you better off than you were four years ago?"* The weekend before the debate the polls showed Carter and Reagan tied, but with this question in the final debate, opinions shifted, decisively. *"If so, vote for four more years of Carter. If not, I suggest another choice,"* Reagan said. On Wednesday, I learn Reagan won the election with a landslide victory, and my misery about American politics sinks to new depths.

"We're going to visit Marian and Jean," Camilla says after dinner. Marian and I don't communicate any better than at the beginning, but I'm still hoping we might connect in some way eventually. The family piles into the car, and Randy and I stay home, side by side on the hearth, alone together in the evening for the first time. Like the sparks in the fire, feelings rise within me. Although Randy and I have spent hours and hours herding, milking, talking, washing dishes, we've never talked about our feelings toward one another. We've surely never touched.

But alone, with tangerine flames dancing in this ancient house in the South of France, I start to feel flushed. Could a setting be more romantic? I smell the burning pine as the wood snaps and pops. Out of nowhere, I wish I could touch him, take him, and caress him.

Oh, God. I'm a twenty-six-year-old woman; and he's so young. He might be seventeen, but he looks thirteen, and that's about how much experience he's had in the world. Still, I sneak a peek over at his blond hair, not combed since being out on the mountain.

I remember being swept away by Herman Raucher's movie, *"Summer of '42"* in high school, when Jennifer O'Neil seduces the teenage boy. Could that be us? Randy and I huddle together like two eggs in a nest, our own little English-speaking world. Do I want to make this seismic shift in our relationship? Get closer?

His delicate fingers, thin, meticulous, clean, flip the pages of *Lost Horizons*—he started it as soon as I finished—and he purses his lips and sips his juice glass of wine as though it were fine bourbon. He ignores me, but I note tension in his back, pink on his neck, and I suspect he feels just like I do. Yes, let's move forward. No, stop. But the pull is strong, I'm melting. No. Best not to act. No, not tonight.

Chapter Six

Travels and Travails

"*Voila!*" Camilla, says. We've arrived in St. Pons, where we first met, my third expedition from the farm in ten weeks. With a lilt in her gait, Camilla bounces like a schoolgirl, her basket swaying on her arm.

First, we enter the *pâtisserie*, where we succumb to scents so tantalizing, so sweet, so delicious, I want to eat every morsel I see. A purple-flowered curtain serves as the back wall, behind which is the shopkeeper's apartment. We face a glass counter with three shelves, each with plates of delicacies, little squares with frosting of pink or white or blue, etched with a *petit* flower, an exquisite artistic masterpiece, as only the French create.

"*Bonjour, Madame,*" says Camilla, her hand flurrying in the classic French greeting.

"Ah," says the broad woman in a *crème*-colored apron tied in the back. "*Bonjour, Madame. Bonjour, Madame.*"

"*Mademoiselle,*" says Camilla.

"Ah, oui. Mademoiselle." Each store keeper stutters when she greets me. Unmarried at twenty-six? I blush.

"Ah, Madame. Ca va bien?" asks Camilla. She speaks with excitement, her voice loud, then soft, in tones of conspiracy. I catch few words. Later, Camilla will tell me of the scandals, the pregnant girls, the abusive husband, the illicit affair, but for now, I just watch. Camilla, her auburn bangs straight and shiny, lifts her chin, and pulls back her shoulders, so her five-foot frame seems to reach the ceiling. Her eyes glisten as her head tips from side to side, animated. Her arms fly in lively conversation. By the time we leave, Camilla has caught up on the gossip and exchanged three mounds of cheese for five bonbons. A success. Yet, she is just beginning.

I follow her next to the *boulangerie,* where, again, she enters like she's a star. *"Bonjour, Madame."* The aroma of fresh bread fills the room like perfume. My eyes land on the *baguettes. Délicieux.*

"Bonjour, Madame. Madame." They nod toward me, then the correction by Camilla, the "what's wrong with you?" look, and finally, "*Mademoiselle.*"

And here the two kisses, one on each cheek. With Camilla's usual flair, she and the shopkeeper begin their lively discourse. With nearly every person we see, the greeting is in the second person singular. In French class, I was taught that *tu* is only used for those with whom one is very familiar. Apparently, Camilla is quite familiar with everyone in town. From store to store, we traverse, my only contribution being, *"Bonjour, Madame,"* or an occasional, "*Merci*" or "*oui*" with a slightly confused smile, hoping "thank you" or "yes" fit the occasion. Still, I relish being with Camilla as she glides from shop to shop like royalty descending on her people.

The next morning, Camilla stands with her hands on her hips. "Randy and Elizabeth," she announces, "we're going to shuck *Castaneas."* Randy's eyes and mine meet. "What's a *Castanea?"* we ask each other in unison.

Camilla wipes off the kitchen table and brings in the two rickety chairs from the *salle à manger* , the only chairs in the entire house, "*Voila*," says Camilla. "Like this." She breaks the hard shell off the large, dark nut, apparently a horse chestnut, although I've never been up on my nuts, and dumps the meat into a bowl.

Randy takes the first shift. When I return from herding at noon, Randy mutters, a nut in one hand, a shell in the other. "Grrrr," he says. "This is bloody awful. First, I tried with my fingers, and next, one knife, and again, another. Look." His hands look mauled, red and scraped.

"Good luck," he says, leaving to herd after noon dinner. I scoot up my chair and begin my work. The point of the knife burrows into the folds of the nut where it should pop in two. Digging in the knife. I wiggle; I prod. Ow! "Whatever doesn't kill you makes you stronger," I think. Whoever came up with that line should be shot.

The French radio drones on and on about God only knows what. I stab my hand on one *Castanea* after another, ripping my hands to pieces all afternoon. Randy and I take turns, day after day the whole long week. We sometimes shell the nuts together. Herding in the bitter wind and rain is hard, but with my raw, scraped hands and knuckles, peeling *Castaneas* is the worst job of all.

A week later, Camilla takes the peeled nuts, boils them, and adds sugar to cook the most delicious sauce. It's like apple sauce with a maple-like taste, and we spread it on bread. With its sweet, tangy, and mellow flavor, it almost melts in my mouth. Yummy. But is it worth it?

You've got to be kidding: No.

The next morning, I bring my chicory-coffee into the *salle à manger* where Jacques chews his bread, listening to the news. "*À toute à l'heure* ," calls Camilla. "We're going to the market." Randy and Camilla leave to sell *fromage de chèvre* in town and purchase the monthly vat of wine from a friend's cellar. The younger children have gone to school, and Michel isn't here. Randy and I never know where our mystery man travels. Like a magician, he appears and disappears without notice.

"*À toute à l'heure* ," I say to Jacques as I head out to herd.

"*Ay liz a bet a,*" he says. "*Pr@f g#ht n*xj.*"

What's that? "Hurry to take the goats out?" I have no idea. I hurry.

"*Allez,*" I call to Elusive, Baby, and the rest. The quick-footed fellows scoot past, toward a plateau hidden in foggy shrubs that reminds me of Japanese black ink paintings, smudges in the mist. I hover by the trees, to protect myself from the mountain winds that become more ferocious each day. Today, they whip my hair across my face like a flag flying on a pole, and flap the pages of my books so it's impossible to read.

Elusive shuffles closer than usual, shrinking her distance to five feet away, while Lucy coos her goat song and Blackbird, a smaller eggplant-colored fellow, clings so closely I smell her sour breath. I scratch Blackbird's head so her bells tinkle.

We missed Halloween, not celebrated in this corner of the world, and now I wonder about Thanksgiving, another holiday Camilla has never heard of. I don't know why I'm surprised. When I mentioned McDonald's, she never heard of that either. "Fast food? I don't get it." Our little farm and village are truly removed from the rest of the world. I visited the McDonald's in Paris, and discovered that its bathroom had a stall with two metal planks on which to squat while your pee went through the middle. *Squat? Really?*

Elusive strains her neck to eat from the branch I hold. She won't step any closer. It's funny how we strain ourselves, challenge ourselves, pick what we're willing to work toward. The other day, Jacques plied me with questions, as he often does. Our conversation about work and routine turned to discussion of Sundays and Sunday routines. "Many families in America," I said, "go to church on Sunday, return for brunch, and savor fresh-roasted coffee while they spend hour after hour reading their local paper and the *New York Times*. They read the news, sports, try the crossword puzzle, and save the magazine section for dessert."

"What?" He shook his head in disbelief. "Americans sit around and read the newspaper all day? We don't have time for that!" Jacques said. "We have too much work to do."

Yes, the *New York Times* symbolizes the lazy American to this Languedoc working man.

My favorite section of NYT (surprise, surprise) reflects my dormant passion to write: *The New York Times Book Review*. A year ago, my roommate in Eugene said, "My mom's writing a book."

Yeah, yeah, yeah, I thought.

"No, it's going to be great!"

"Sure, Katy," I said, biting into my tofu-salsa sandwich.

"No, really, she's been doing research for years."

I wiped my mouth, took another bite, and leafed through a copy of *Rolling Stone*. "Uh-huh."

This August, right before I flew to Europe, I opened the *NYT Book Review*. There, on the front page, was a review of Katy's mother's book. I didn't believe it at first. I had to read the fine print. "Author from Portland, Oregon." OREGON! New Yorkers can't find Oregon on a map, nonetheless pronounce it! But there it was, Jean Auel's book, *The Clan of the Cave Bear*. My eyes popped to see this, the pinnacle of success for an American writer, a front-page *New York Times Book Review*. And Katy's mom had done it! I felt a tiny pinprick of hope. Maybe I will go to Paris to be a writer, like I always dreamed. And so I went. And here I am, detoured in the mountains of Languedoc.

The winds feel like grains of sandpaper on my cheeks. "*Allez,*" I call, beckoning the goats. "Time for my noon dinner."

"*Bonjour,*" I say, when I enter the house. Even in the silence, I sense anger. The air feels thick. Jacques is alone. I gulp. What's wrong? Jacques sits erect on his chair, his forehead wrinkled like a bulldog, and he points his finger at me. "You're late!"

"But there wasn't a problem," I say. Oh, my naiveté. It takes a moment to realize how furious he is. "I just didn't look at my watch." Truth is, I was too absorbed thinking. Just thinking, I'd lost track of time, but it's not such a big deal, is it?

Rigid in his chair, Jacques taps his foot in a syncopated rhythm. He's never been mad at me like this, never raged like he does with Michel. I freeze, wondering what I've done wrong besides being a little late for the noon meal. A chill runs up my spine. I serve the bread and the peppery potato leek soup. The only sound is "*Louisianne,*" which has progressed in history to the year 1808, soon after Jefferson bought Louisiana from Napoleon.

I serve Jacques his coffee. "*Voila*," I say, worried. Now he taps his foot even harder, his eyes like iron, unforgiving. He scrapes his chair on the cement floor, sounding like a nail on a blackboard, reaching for his sugar from the hutch. I've forgotten to give it to him, as I often do. I jump and hand it to him.

The fire smokes from the green oak limbs. I'm even more anxious I'll lose my job. I'm so frustrated about all the years I studied French, yet how little I understand. Sure, I can say and hear more French than when I first arrived, but I still miss so much. Jacques' anger touches a reservoir deep within me, emotions I've buried, feelings that once triggered my overeating: I screwed up.

I've grown so much since I've been here, and I usually feel good about myself. But not now. I flash on Garner.

Even though we came from opposite worlds, we're tied together with the notion that deep, deep inside us, we're a piece of shit. On some level we're smart, but on another we are…what?... confused at best.

When Jacques' radio program ends, I ask, "Should I wash the dishes or do we milk the goats now?"

"There's not enough time to milk the goats." Finally, I put it all together. Jacques felt sick this morning, so we didn't milk the goats then. Apparently, what he'd said to me after breakfast was, "Bring back the goats early, so we can milk them before dinner because I have an appointment right afterwards." I whip through the dishes, bummed. I never discover where he is running off to. I hustle to the barn for my afternoon shift.

The following morning, Camilla is cheerful at breakfast, calling, "*Allez, Ay liz a bet a.*" As in, "let's go somewhere, for some reason." Oh, good. I need a change of scene. Camilla drives me to an ancient building reminiscent of the police station in *Casablanca* with slimy, reeking mildew. Our footsteps pound the cavernous hallway of the *gendarmerie*, the police station. Camilla opens a door twice as tall as we are, and we enter an office where the *gendarme* poses rigidly behind a broad wooden desk. The door slams behind us. Dressed in his black uniform with gold epaulettes, he observes us with dull eyes, rapping his cigarette on an ashtray that overflows with smoldering butts.

He speaks to Camilla in a gruff, guttural voice, but I understand nothing as Camilla and he flail their hands like they're charging into battle with voices raised. I'm like a silent filmgoer watching: his jaw tightens, narrow nose expands, contracts. Camilla pushes her glasses up her nose, holds onto her armrests so tightly that her veins protrude from her hands. Momentary silence. He holds the power. She beseeches. He won't push her too far. They are acquaintances, friends. Now their voices become louder, turn to laughter and he pushes back his chair, stands, and dismisses us. Camilla clutches her purse and I follow her down the dungeon-like corridor, back to the car where she explains what just transpired, but I can't put meaning into her words. I need to study my French lessons with more rigor!

A week later, she announces, "*Ay liz a bet a,* you're going to Spain!" Spain?! Yahoo! A mini-adventure! I'm not sure why I'm going, but wonder if our trip to the *gendarme* concerned my work visa. All I know for certain is that I need to get my passport stamped, and in order to do so, I must leave France.

"You'll go by train to Spain," Camilla says, "and turn around and come back. We'll pay for it." A paid vacation! I can hardly wait. Yes, traveling through France was fun, challenging, but I understood a tad of French. Remnants of past *Français* lessons swam in the bottom of my brain. But Spanish? I know no Spanish. None. The fact that half my hometown in Holyoke, Massachusetts now speaks Spanish makes me laugh, is ironic, but doesn't help me any. Traveling through Spain excites me, and I trust I'll manage okay. I travel well. When I'm on the road, I feel a powerful sense of spirit, like She or He or Whoever, guides me safely.

Yes, I've had some scares, but still, travel strengthens my spirituality, which may be why I love it so.

Exhilarated, I imagine riding a train to Barcelona. I think of cranberry velvet capes on matadors, and bulls, and Hemingway—I confuse Barcelona with Pamplona—and flamenco guitars playing in the street. A few days later, Camilla says, "*Non.*"

"*Non?*"

"No," says Camilla. "There's been a change of plans." I deflate. "We're going to drive you. Kathy's parents will lend us their car. We'll go on Sunday."

So much for the train. But still, Spain!

The day arrives with a golden sunrise spreading lavender streaks across the sky. I wave goodbye to our four-home village and chuckle at the situations I get myself into. We aren't borrowing Kathy's parents' car. No, Kathy's parents are going, too. But who is Kathy? I have no idea. I have no idea who Kathy is, but whoever she is, the first thing Mr. Kathy says when he meets me is, "France is better than America. Right?" Oh, brother.

Mr. Kathy, dressed in a blue wool coat and cap with black rim, navigates the familiar corkscrew curves on our barely two-lane road. He speaks to Jacques, sitting next to him, with a voice of authority, while he waggles his hand like he's quite the important fellow. Mrs. Kathy sits with Camilla and me in the back with her freshly coiffed hair—how do these French women stay so beautiful in city or country?—and bright cobalt eyes that glint as she converses with Camilla. The purple sky melts to pink, then blue. We pass hills and steel-colored boulders until we reach Beziers, the closest city to our farm, an hour and a half east. Jacques, riding up front, twists around eagerly to explain to me that Beziers was an important city hundreds, even thousands of years ago, since it's situated on the main route stretching east from Italy, around the Mediterranean through France, and south to Spain. Ancient Romans coming from Italy walked and rode this road around the Mediterranean from the east, and Africans, Saracens, and Spaniards came up from the south. This is the site of the Albigensian Crusade, where armies in the name of the Pope, decimated the entire population.

Jacques points to the Saint-Nazaire Cathedral, high on the hill, facing south. Hundreds of years ago, citizens could view invaders from as far south as Morocco. The narrow, windy streets are lined with stone buildings, built during the past five centuries, all mixed together. Archeologists believe Beziers, now with a population of 60,000, was originally occupied as early as the Stone Age, around 9500 BCE. I cannot fathom humans living nearly ten thousand years before Jesus Christ.

The city and buildings fall behind us and the country opens to green pastures dotted with French bulls, *terreau*, running wild, the ones bullfighters taunt in arenas. Large horses, with huge grey snouts, pose in fields, erect with grandeur. *"Voila,"* says Jacques, excited. *"Les Camargues."* These wild Camargues exude a majestic air. They gallop so gracefully, it seems they might rise from the ground and fly. I'm awed by the magnificent beasts. Scrunched in the backseat against the window, I have two visions. Unlike daydreams, they're pictures in my mind. In one, I ride horseback, cantering along the ocean, and in another, I'm at the site of a gypsy festival by the sea. Both visions come true several months later. I've become more intuitive than ever before, living so close to nature. My dreams are vivid, but I've never before experienced such a clear, daytime vision.

In a few hours we reach the border of Spain where each of our passports is stamped. Mission accomplished. My pal, Mr. Kathy, drives into a Spanish village where locals dress in worn clothes, wrinkled and aged like their faces. They barter at the market square, shouting, tossing their hands in the air like they're giving vivacious speeches. We sit on plastic chairs at an outdoor café where I watch a little girl with hair loosely falling off her shoulders, her socks dirty yellow, her voice sweet, lilting like a Spanish song. The toasty *frites* smell enticing, but I order a strawberry crepe that tastes like the fruit was picked from the garden this morning. From the smoke of the cigarettes to the fragrances of the exquisite food, my senses are delighted.

I savor my *café con leche,* delicious coffee with no chicory adding acid to the flavor. So, so, SO delicious. Eugene, Oregon discovered lattes at the same time the first Starbucks appeared in Seattle in 1971. For years I drank lattes. I drank double-tall lattes, and during exam week, it was triple tall lattes for me.

I spot a small stand across the street. "One moment," I say. Lured by newspapers, I head to the vendor who sells papers from Barcelona, Madrid, Paris, Rome, and, *Voila!* Gold! *The International Herald Tribune!* My favorite of all newspapers: all the news that's fit to print in eight short pages of this *New York Times* international newspaper. All these weeks I've been trying to decipher the French radio, trying to understand what's going on in the world, and here it is in brief, intelligent English. I cling to the paper, thrilled, ecstatic to read the goings-on in America and the rest of the world.

As we head north, back home again, Jacques turns to me. "*Voila, les Camargues,*" and "*Voila, les montagnes,*" and "*Voila, le soleil.*"

"*Ah, oui,*" I respond, my nose glued to the *Tribune.* Jacques' face reddens as though personally offended. "Here you are in Spain, and you're reading a damn newspaper?"

Still, I read.

We pass the border again. Our passports are stamped again. It's now legal for me to continue working in France.

And still, I read.

Up in the hills the next morning, Baby's scratchy tongue tickles my palm. Randy and I named about half of the goats, unlike the sheep, whom I basically ignore, and who ignore me. Ma Rosa, who still bugs me, grows larger and larger with her unborn calf. I pet Baby like a puppy dog, hold her face with two hands before I rub under chin.

With my journal in my lap, ready to write, I gaze across the acres of field and rocks chewing my pen, thinking about George Eliot's *Adam Bede*, my latest book. It's like a morality play where good and bad collide. What about "good" and "bad" feelings? What is the deal with labeling feelings anyway? There is perhaps, no better job for a wondering philosophy major like me than goat herding.

Why do "fun" feelings, like "good" or "happy," seem so shallow? Why does sadness, sorrow, and grief seem deeper, more significant? As though they're more important emotions? As though they reach more deeply into one's soul?

Sadness and loneliness. Do I actually prefer these dark feelings to those of superficial happiness?

I think back to a moment of kindness—kindness that once reached as deeply as any grief. One evening in Eugene, I asked my friend Ted, a real friend even though I weighed 180 pounds, "What do you think about my being so overweight?" It took courage to ask. I knew he'd be honest. I braced for, "I think you're a pig, ugly, pitiful." I felt the humidity of the summer evening, heard the crickets chirping in the smoldering heat. "Disgusting," perhaps he'd say.

Finally, he spoke. He astounded me, floored me. "I wonder why," he said. "I wonder why you are so overweight."

I drew in a breath, exhaled it slowly. Then, another. Relief. Those words were the kindest ever spoken. Instead of judging me, he wondered *why*. During that hot evening in Eugene, gratitude poured from my heart. That's when I learned, kindness can reach as deeply as sorrow.

But what about "feeling good?" It's a sin to feel good, right? According to someone's religious book. Catholics? And yet in reality, isn't that all anyone ever wants? To feel good? Doesn't a saint feel good when he or she sacrifices, does good for others, and is kind and loving? Just as a greedy, stingy bastard feels good by stealing a million dollars off the backs of the poor, while he lives in his palace in Bimini? Is the saint better than the crook? I think so. But who am I to judge? As good as anyone else, I suppose.

Perched on my rock with my journal on my knees, I gaze at Grand Marnier with her butterscotch coat, soft and shiny. I first heard the concept of "positive" and "negative" energy in relation to thoughts and emotions, when, on a hitchhiking trip, I stopped with a fellow traveler in Malibu to follow the Monarch butterflies fluttering overhead on their annual migration to Mexico.

Positive or negative. I didn't grasp the idea at first. "John is an asshole." A negative thought. "It's a beautiful day." Positive. I finally understood, but there was a problem with the concept. If we can choose whether we think positively or negatively, we have a great deal of personal power. Many people would prefer to blame others, rather than accept that personal responsibility.

Grand Marnier arches her back with her legs up the tree to chomp as many leaves as she can fit in her mouth. "Feeling good" might not feel like a deep emotion, but yes, it's worthwhile to make myself feel happy, to make others happy, to spread positive energy. My old Kantian professor once said, "Artists think they need to feel angst, that being miserable is a core requirement for creativity and artistic endeavor. Untrue! Haydn, for example, was extremely happy."

After noon dinner, I add wood to the kitchen cooking stove. I wash the cheese forms and make *fromage de chèvre*, listening to Jerry Garcia singing *Uncle John's Band.* It's fairly warm, my task is easy, and I love my music. Life is good.

Good, that is, until the end of the afternoon, when Randy bursts in, pounding the door against the wall. "It's bloody awful how the Fontaines treat their goats! And the dogs!" His eyes bulge as he rants. "The dogs are a bloody nuisance. Natasha cut a huge gash in Hairy's ankle. They shouldn't have goats."

I fiddle with the wood in the stove, blow on the coals, and close the black iron door, gritting my teeth. I want to scream. "Shut up! No one can be as perfect as you!" His criticisms are driving me crazy. And lately, he's more irritable than ever. I love Randy with complicated feelings. Not like how I love Garner, of course. But, these criticisms! I say nothing as he marches into the *salle à manger*.

At supper Marie and Louis argue, as usual. Marie slugs Louis, and he hits her back. "Stop it, Marie!" shouts Camilla, who, as always, sides with Louis.

"You don't see Randy and *Ay liz a bet a* fighting, or me and your mother acting like that," Jacques says. Nice try. No effect. Jacques usually withdraws from the dinner table family dynamics. Physically distant, he rarely kisses or hugs or touches the children, or even Camilla, for that matter.

After supper, I find the embroidery that I bought in town and begin with a hand towel. Randy remains in his habitual stance: his back to the hissing fire, arms behind him with fingers locked, staring at the walls. His tiny mouth tightens. Something, more than how the Fontaines treat their animals, bothers him. I used to worry the Fontaines would let one of us go. Now I worry Randy will leave on his own.

Suddenly inspired, I say, "Hey Randy, I've got extra embroidery. Would you like some?"

He stares at my outstretched hands. "Aulright." I show him different color threads and hand him a needle and the scissors. He dives in. Ten minutes later, he asks, "How do you like these stitches?"

"Nice," I say. He's suddenly humming as he dips his needle in and out of the towel he's sewing. Phew.

Randy's cheerfulness does not last long. First one week, then the next, he hangs his head, his mouth taut, no longer cracking his dry Australian jokes. The embroidery helped, but he's still in a funk. I want to shake him out of it. "Marie." I pull her aside after dinner. "Want to help me make Randy feel better? Let's bring him breakfast in bed?"

"Oui!" She claps her hands, excited for our secret conspiracy. The next morning, we rise quietly. I thread pieces of bread on a stick and roast them over the fire in *the salle à manger* 'til the whole room smells of half-burned toast. Marie slaps fresh jam on one slice, and butter, which melts right away, on the other, while I pour warm milk into a bowl and place it on a tray. Marie fills a cup with chicory, and I add a glass with the last red poppy from outside the door. Marie giggles as I kneel at the top of the ladder. She reaches up, trying not to tip the tray, and hands it to me.

We approach the closed curtain that separates the boys from Camilla and Jacques. "Randy," I call. "*Bonjour,* Randy.

We've got something for you." I lift the curtain to find the largest grin I've ever seen.

In shock, Randy fluffs his pillow against the wall and sits up. "Why, thank you" he says in his usual polite manner. He's dumbfounded.

Between the embroidery and breakfast in bed, Randy emerges from his misery, like a burden lifts from his shoulders. At least for awhile.

A day later, after herding, I find Marian in the kitchen, her face paler than usual. "Marian, what's wrong? What happened?" A sense of doom, of sorrow, permeates the house. Marian responds, but I do not understand. Camilla enters, speaking more slowly. An earthquake measuring 6.89 on the Richter scale has hit Irpinia, Southern Italy. Centered in the village of Conza, it's only about five hundred miles away. It's like living in Massachusetts and finding out Maine had been hit. The injury count is updated on the radio: 2,900 people killed, 10,000 injured, and 300,000 homeless.

Marian asks Camilla what she needs help with. Hearing "leeks," Marian immediately takes a bucket out to the water truck outside the kitchen door, washes garden dirt off the leeks, and begins to chop. Fundamental to this Languedoc culture is work. The answer to any question about the meaning of life is work. Everyone works, everyone helps.

I wonder once again how long Marian has lived around here, and what she did before she came to this remote part of the world. How long have she and Jean been married? I don't ask though, not only because I'm a little star-struck as she floats in and out of our lives, but because we still barely understand each other.

While she dumps the leeks in the soup and I chop onions, she asks, "How long are you staying here?"

"Until spring," I say. Her smile seems tender. The light shining through the dusty window softens her cheeks, her nose, her mouth. I feel awkward, and I think she does too, like two lovers who've faced an impasse. What more is to be said? We think of nothing.

Yesterday's sunshine was an aberration, a tease. The cold rains and sharp winds of the previous weeks return with a vengeance. The thrill of goat herding is gone.

Fewer and fewer of the goats have milk, so we milk just once a day. It takes little time. I committed to stay through the winter, knowing it would be harsh, but I've never felt this kind of raw cold, even during frigid New England winters. The water tank freezes. Now we must hike to a spring a quarter of a mile up a hill to fetch water.

I button my coat in the kitchen, ready to head to the barn. "Happy Thanksgiving," Marie says to me, giggling, her eyes sparkling with a touch of mischief. She loves to show off her English, since she's the only Fontaine who can speak even a smattering. She learned about the holiday in school.

"Qu'est que ce?" asks Camilla. What's that?

"Thanksgiving's a big holiday in America. It celebrates the Pilgrims, the first Americans (according to people from Massachusetts) to survive the cold winter with the help of the Indians. Families get together, mostly just to eat—

turkey, stuffing, pumpkin pie, mince pie. There's no work or school."

"Ahh," says Camilla. She pokes the wood in the stove, and I wrap myself in scarves and mittens, a hat, heavy boots, and march out the door. So much for Thanksgiving.

A few days later, the rusty, brown tractor gurgles and grumbles, and chugs around the back of the house. Jacques sits high on its broken seat, his grey pants frayed at the knee, and waits for me to hop up to help him collect that most precious of commodities, firewood, which equals heat for the house and fuel for the stove. The tractor pulls an ancient wagon with broken wood sides, partially caved in. I hop on, holding on for dear life, for my first tractor ride ever. We rattle up the road, through the hills, bouncing up and down, thud, thud, thud on the uneven wheels along the pathway, beyond the fresh-smelling oak trees where we herd the goats. I laugh as we go along, calling to Natasha who bounds behind us. I'm as excited as if I were at Disneyland, but instead of lights, rides, and flashy colors, I have a muddy road, rocks, and bushes. What would the other French farmers think about an adult woman getting such a kick out of her first tractor ride?

After driving up, down, and around, we jerk to a stop. Jacques and I jump off, and he points to the scattered limbs, indicating I'm to gather branches and logs. I gather as many boughs as possible and lug them over to the tractor. We find fallen trees, almost as large as Jacques, which we tie with a metal chain and rope and together, yank them up by the roots. I feel muscles I never knew I had. My body is strong and flexible and I feel so alive, tickled with this adventure, like a female, adult Huck Finn.

We load the smaller trees, scraping our arms and hands, piling the wood, grateful for the sun that peeks through the grey sky, warming the chilly air. I feel light in my head from the altitude. More and more wood is stacked in the wagon until even one more twig would surely fall off. Jacques wrenches the throttle, the tractor makes a grunt and a lurch, and he starts to drive home. Though this escapade is fun for me, it's an absolute necessity for the Fontaines, because without this wood, our house would be freezing, like the water in the tank we can no longer use. I'm guessing my joy in this work, which is routine for the Fontaines, brings joy to the whole household.

Natasha and I trail behind the wagon like Timmy with Lassie, from the old TV show. Jacques stops the tractor and turns his wind-worn face to me. "Do you want to sit on top of the branches on the wagon?" The pile of branches and roots look wobbly, not at all sturdy, so I climb on top of the fender of the big tractor wheel, feeling the strong muscles in my arms and legs. It's true what they say about the connection between mind and body. The more alive my body becomes, the more alive my spirit becomes, and the more I believe in myself.

Part II. Wisdom and Compassion

"There is no such thing as a simple act of compassion or an inconsequential act of service. Everything we do for another person has infinite consequences."

Caroline Myss, Mountains and Memories

Part II. Wisdom and Compassion

Chapter Seven
The Veterinarian

The rabbit stew tastes both sweet and tart, as long as I don't remember that brown twitching nose and those coal-black eyes which, just this morning, blinked at me while I did my business on the planks of *la toilette.* At supper Jacques breaks the silence. "The veterinarian is coming tomorrow," he says between bites.

"Ah, bon!" Marie and Louis shout, dancing around the table. Randy and I eye each other. Why the excitement?

The next morning, Mr. Bawdy, who looks like a homeless fellow from under a Parisian bridge with his unkempt hair and bulging belly, storms into the *salle à manger,* apparently to help with the vet's visit. "Randy," I whisper. "What's going on?"

"I haven't a clue," he says, in his usual monotone voice. Randy never approves of anything the Fontaines do, and probably never will, but the jury's out on this occasion, because we have no idea what's happening, only that the kids are talking fast, Bawdy is hollering, Camilla is wiping her hands on her apron, and now we're all charging like an army down to the barn. Jacques lugs open the barn door, we dismantle the partitions that separate the animals, and out they all soar, running, kicking up the musk-scented dirt, baaing, snorting and cooing around and around in wild chaos while everyone screams and yells.

Jacques calls, "*Allez, allez,*" flinging his hands in futility while Marie and Louis dash every which way, and filthy Bawdy thrashes his hand, shouting, scaring the goats and sheep, so that instead of assembling into a neat little group (which is the goal), they all scatter even more. Jacques fires off directions, words tumbling rapidly like machine gun fire, but nobody listens. The sheep baa louder; Ma Rosa snorts; the goats flick their little tails; and Marie and Louis run here and there, while Bawdy shouts like a buffoon, and Randy chuckles in his understated Australian way, like an impassive observer with his thin lips turning into the slightest of smiles at this crazy spectacle.

Finally, the goats settle down, more or less, in a confined area, while Bawdy hollers who knows what. Randy and I hush the animals, petting their heads, and speaking softly. Jacques hands us markers. "Write numbers on the back of their rumps," he says, so we take the markers and write: 1, 2, and on through 42, so now our little herd looks like a football line-up, primed for the doc. One by one, the vet examines their ears, their teeth, feels their stomachs, and looks at their hooves, while we try to keep the rest of the herd in line. He gives them shots and inoculations and a clean bill of health.

Randy calls the little football team up the hills, while I brush off my hands, ready to scoop up the buckets for water. "*Ay liz a bet a*," Camilla asks. "Would you like to go into town?" Leave the farm, again? For a fourth time in four months? Absolutely.

Our tin car swerves the mountain roads with the cool winds sweeping my face, and I wonder if my French has improved since my last trip. I've studied most every day with my book and tape player, repeating the lessons over and over. I even had an "ahaa" moment—one night when I listened to my French cassette tape in bed with earphones. I suddenly recognized a rhythm, a flow, the cadence of the French language.

In fact, one day I felt so mighty darned pleased with how much I'd learned, I thought I'd show off. At dinner, I ripped some bread from the baguette in the basket, preparing for my big moment. I cleared my throat, puffed my chest a smidgen, smiled, and repeated a French sentence I learned from my book. "When I go into town I'll ask for everything I need from the kind store keeper."

"Pshaw." Jacques said, not looking up from his soup. "They talk like that in Paris. We don't talk like that here."

Oh, yeah. We're a long way from Paris.

When we arrive on my second visit to town, Camilla collects her basket of cheese to sell and barter. "You can do your errands, while I do mine," she says as she sets off in one direction, while I head in another. With the warm sun reflecting against the shop windows, I feel a sense of freedom, alone in this French village, with my newfound language skills, albeit not as terrific as I wish they were. I enter the first shop to the tinkle of bells, alerting the storekeeper, a beefy woman with a broad smile and thick cheeks, who emerges from her apartment in the back of the shop.

"*Bonjour, Madame,*" I say, and continue in French. "Some toothpaste, please."

"Ah, Bonjour, Mademoiselle. Voila!" She hands me toothpaste. She understands! I can speak!

"Merci, bien," I say. Thank you so much.

And to the next shop. "*Bonjour, Madame.*"

"Bonjour, Mademoiselle." How are you? Very well, and you? Very well. May I please have some embroidery? Certainly. Yes! Embroidery. I've been so humbled by Jacques' comment, that the response of the shopkeepers delights me. I've made progress!

The day after our trip to town, Split-Infinitive leads the herd past Jacques' Camargues. With their huge, grey haunches and platinum box noses, they whisk their heads from side to side. To me, they epitomize grace.

Horses scared me since I was in kindergarten, when my family rented a summer house on Cape Cod. My sister, three years older, and I meandered down a lane edged with tall grass, the air smelling like the sea. "Look," she said, pointing to a pasture a bit further down the road. A big—*enormous* to my five-year-old eyes— horse poked his nose through a wire fence. My sister adored all horses, and rubbed his huge, soft nose while he whinnied and nuzzled her. Not wanting to be a fraidy-cat, I held one hand behind my back, and hesitantly stroked the giant nose. In a flash, the horse flicked his head and opened his thick lips, baring his yellow teeth, and nipped my tiny arm. I raced home, more frightened than hurt, but the dread of horses stuck with me. I've ridden since, taken horseback riding lessons, but never with enthusiasm.

Out in the Fontaines' fields, though, Jacques' Camargues captivate me, enchant me in a way I can't put my finger on. "Camilla," I ask, back at the house, "May I ride the horses?"

I've been reading another book about enduring the brutal, arid heat in the deadly Australian outback, and it makes me want to face challenges, to face my fears. While I might not survive the outback, surely I can overcome the trepidation of horses. This much I've figured out—if I want to get rid of self-doubt, I need to face my fear.

"Of course, you can ride," says Camilla. On my next day off, Jacques shows me how to put on the bridle and saddle. I clench my foot in the stirrup and with a huge heave up, I land on the enormous beast, feeling lumps in my throat as I swallow my worry.

The horse trots out of the barn, and I think about how horses sense fear, and the more I think about them sensing my fear, the more terrified I feel. My childhood English riding lessons didn't prepare me for ropes as reins and giant stirrups to flop my legs in. My horse begins to trot, and I don't know if I'm supposed to post or not, but I hold onto the saddle horn and stay within sight of the barn. He starts to canter, or is it just a plain run, and my legs flop like a rag doll holding on for dear life until I steer him back to the barn.

OK. I've ridden a Camargue. Check that off the list. No need for that again.

November gives way to December, and each day we freeze a little more. I am cold all the time, and no matter how many layers of long underwear, shirts, sweaters, coats I wear, no matter how close to the fire I sit, I cannot shake the chill. To endure the ghastly winds, lashing snow, and frigid temperatures, we herd for only two hours in the morning, two in the afternoon.

Out with the herd in a snowstorm, I'm surrounded by blinding white, with only three feet of visibility. "*Allez,*" I call, hoping my goats won't wander off. They won't. Like scared children, they stick to me, their guardian in this storm. My gloved hands sink into my torn jacket pocket, searching for warmth. My knees lock. I ignore my breath, which resembles an icy San Francisco fog. I should move my feet, but I can't. My nose and ears burn with cold, and I feel like crying. The goats' bells ring lightly. How will these guys find enough to eat from these scrappy, windblown trees? Why are we even out here in this heinous weather?

It's like Dr. Zhivago's Siberian winter—white snow and stick trees stretch on mercilessly, as far as the eye can see. Are my toes frostbitten, like that time I skied at Killington when my friends, worried about the white streaks on my cheeks, grabbed my ski poles and pulled me down the slope? I should hop or jump. My mind feels fuzzy. I must rouse myself.

A sharp wind claws my face and shrieks like a rabid dog, and I think about last night, sitting on the broad stone hearth, the fire warming my back when I read a damp letter from my friend, Jeri, in Eugene. "Hey, Elizabeth," she wrote, "I think of you on the thyme-covered hills, looking east to the Mediterranean and South to the Pyrenees. Your life herding goats and sheep is sooo romantic!" I blink and brush the tiny icicles off my lashes. Romantic? *This is romantic?*

Too cold to sit or read, I sing with my goats, belting out the first two lines of every song I know, like John Candy in *Canadian Bacon* when he chants Bruce Springsteen's, "BORN in the USA!! Born in the USA!" Blank, he can't remember any more lines. So again, "Born in the USA!" I check my watch every four minutes, wiggling my toes so they won't freeze, praying please, please let it be time to go in.

On the hills the following day, Baby coils around my calf while the rest of the herd scrounges for a leaf here, an unburied nut there. My mind wanders. What's going on between Randy and me and our "pleasant," undefined relationship? I spend more time with him than, perhaps, anyone before in my life outside my family. We know the meaning of each glance, each gesture, each intoned word, and yet, he's so, so young. We're in that nowhere-land between friend and lover, brother and mate. Where will this strange friendship lead? I still dream of Garner, whom I haven't heard from since I left America. I've just got to shake that Garner out of my head!

I huddle near a cluster of boulders with my goats and sheep. In my current book, *Adam Bede*, George Eliot describes peasants who live close to the earth, saying they represent "human nature in its purest form." Diana, a major character in *Adam Bede*, dies as a "near saint," because she's conflicted over her desire for a man and her desire to have a relationship with God. At least that's how I interpret the story. Her struggle reminds me of my own pull toward Garner, and the opposite pull toward living more spiritually, detached from an unhealthy relationship. I believe in something greater than myself. Call it nature, call it God, but this connection is the essence of a better life. I feel this union with nature, and yet, I surely don't possess Diana's quality of faith.

Eliot's character in *Bede* says, "Sit quietly and think of people in distress and ask for God's help for them." While Baby nibbles snowy nuts from my hand, I meditate with a prayer and focus on distressed people, victims of the Italian earthquake, emulating *Bede*.

Was Eliot right? Are people who live closest to the land the "purest?" If so, these peasants in the mountains of the South of France, Camilla and Jacques, Marian and Jean, are the purest yet.

I trust Garner, not for his fidelity or even his honesty, but because he is true to himself. He wears no airs. He grew up with his grandfather, living in a shack with plastic on the windows, cold; half-blind with no glasses. His high school girlfriend loved him, and dumped him because of his drinking.

He drew beautifully with pen and ink, and sketched me an ancient Indian with an eagle flying from his hair. Friends tried to sober him up, to introduce him to other artists, friends who went to Oxford and Vassar, who recognized a genius underneath a marred and tarnished life. All efforts were to no avail.

Climbing a narrow path high on the mountainside, past snow piled halfway up the small trees, I fix my eyes on the dell below. I imagine Garner appearing, his face too cute, too sweet for his swagger, the swagger I'd recognize anywhere.

I rub Baby's damp fur and squint as though, if I stare long enough, hope hard enough, I'll conjure up Garner, and he'll live with us through this stormy winter. But, no matter how many times I squeeze my eyes or wish or pray, he remains an apparition. I can accept that the world is unfair, but no, not that love is unfair—that he can love me, and I him, but it's not good for either of us. I don't know if my love toward Garner is real, or pure, but compared to him, the rest of the world bores me.

Still, if I stayed with Garner, I'd be like a moth circling a light, closer and closer, until zzzzt! I'd fry myself on the bulb. That's what it's like to love a heavy drinker, I was told. You lose your belief in yourself, and you lose your confidence, your ambition, and your peace of mind, because all your efforts aim to fix him, to make him be the man you know he could be. "Walk away or go down in flames with the person you love." That's what I learned in those workshops I attended back in Eugene. I walked away. I walked away from an obsession and am a better woman for it. And yet still, he haunts me.

I count the goats before I head back to the barn. Where's Georgia? Oh, no. Not again. She wandered away from the herd before, and Randy believes she has dementia. Usually, we find her down at the barn, but sometimes we have to search for her after dark. I call over and over, "*Allez! Allez!*" No Georgia.

Back at the house, I smell the pepper in tonight's potato soup and hear the "click, click, click" of hooves. "Camilla found Georgia down by the barn." Randy says. "She brought her in for one last moment of comfort." I tilt my head, questioning. Georgia's hooves sound like hammers, clamping nails on the cement floor. "She's too old," Randy says.

Oooh. Georgia is ancient. She'll be killed. We need to kill her. We'll be killing goats all year. But, Georgia is almost a friend, and my stomach turns.

"Randy," says Camilla. "Will you take her down to the barn?"

"I'm coming, too." I say to Randy. "I eat the goats, after all. I should take responsibility for killing them, too." My voice trembles.

Jacques ties Georgia to a post. In the back of the barn, a few goats brush against their rope partitions and snort. Randy holds Georgia's head. Jacques and I hold her body, while Camilla takes a sharp knife and, with a surgeon's skill slits her throat, precisely pulling the knife from left to right so blood gushes out, into the pan that Jacques holds under the goat's neck. My stomach pitches and my eyes mist. I say a prayer for her spirit, and focus my eyes on her spilt hooves and the red drops that splatter on to them. Unlike Randy and me, the Fontaines never name their goats. As they untie the carcass, I understand why.

Randy stomps out of the barn, and I chase him through the snow. "That was bloody awful!" he says, shaking his head and squeezing his fist until its white.

"What?"

"The blood!" Scorn punctuates his voice. "Cutting her neck and draining her blood is far more painful than just killing. That's a horrid way to die. The only reason they killed her that way is because people like to eat white meat instead of dark." Randy seethes. "There's no need to put her through that much pain!" I shudder. The things I never knew.

Jacques and Camilla haul the carcass back to the *salle à manger* , flop it on the table, and skin the goat. Jacques hangs the hide up to dry. Next, he slashes the body, most of which will become added to stew.

Time for supper. Marie wipes dead Georgia's blood off the table; Randy sets the silverware; and I bring the plates. Yes, this is an all purpose table. Let's eat.

What can you do with a dead goat? Far more than I would guess. The following evening, Camilla cooks soup for dinner. I glance at the head in the pot and scream, "Goat's Head Soup!" Michel is the only rocker of our little group, the only one who can appreciate the Rolling Stones album. The meal freaks me out at first, but after living with the Fontaines for three months, it's not so weird after all. I quickly write to Susannah, "You'll never believe it! We had goat's head soup for dinner!"

Goat stew is a staple, of course, magnificent with red wine, native thyme, and potatoes. Next, the brains: black little urchins that look like maggots. Even the kids scrunch their noses. I bite a tad of the tiny, black wormy things and gag. Disgusting! That night, the kids and I stick to bread and milk, while Camilla, Randy, and Jacques enjoy (Yuck! Yuck!) the brains.

Finally, we make sausage. Every ounce of leftover meat is churned in a grinder. We take the skin off the intestines, tie a knot to the bottom like we might an old stocking, and stuff it with left over goat organs, onions, and herbs. With the fire snapping branches, we all sit around the table stuffing intestine sleeves. Jacques carefully hangs each stuffed sausage from a stick. He'll dry them in the *fromagerie*. "Aren't they pretty?" he asks.

I laugh. "No, I don't think so; I think they're gross."

I notice a look of hurt in his eye. I realize he really does see beauty. I study them again. The sausages hang symmetrically with even spaces between each them.

"They look like bells," he says.

Why, yes, they do. They sort of are lovely, in fact. And perhaps, I think as I admire Jacques' bells, Eliot is right. These people living closest to the earth are the purest. The ugly sausages transform to beauty right before my eyes.

Chapter Eight

The Gift

With dirt coating my body and hair from days and days of herding in muddy snow, I can't put off my weekly bath. Since the water tank in front of the house has long since frozen, I lug two buckets on a frosty night past the barn, up a path slick with snow and ice, to a spring in a stone crevice. A handmade wooden plug sticks in *the source,* a spring of water between the rocks. I set my flashlight on a ledge and fill the two pails with water. While mountain winds slash my face, I pull the plug and unleash the water, as if from a faucet. That is, a faucet a quarter-mile from the house.

With my buckets filled as high as possible, I tug on the handles and, as steadily as I can, sidestepping so not to fall, I cart them filled to the brim without spilling a drop. Once home, I add more wood to the fire in the *salle à manger* , heat the water, and pour it into a bucket in the kitchen near the hot wood stove. I strip off my clothes, cover myself with a towel, position myself on a chair in the kitchen, and rub the rough washcloth over my legs, my stomach, my breasts. I sympathize with Festus who, in the show *Gunsmoke,* sat with his knees to his chin in a half-barrel, long brush in hand and cowboy hat on his head, complaining every moment of his bath. The water is cold and dirty before I'm halfway through, and I keep checking the door for some unsuspecting neighbor who might drop by. Dried and dressed, I pour more boiling water in the bucket on the table, and set an empty one at my feet. "Randy?" I call. Randy pours the water through my hair, I massage in the shampoo, and he rinses with a few cups of water, which are supposed to go from the cup, through my hair, to the empty bucket on the floor. Theoretically.

The rinse water, in fact, rarely catches the shampoo and usually, I'm left with soapy hair, a wet shirt, a wet towel, and a cement floor to mop, all a far cry from my old luxurious, long-soaking baths, half meditation, all comfort that I still dream about most every night. I hang the mop on a hook, and Camilla bounds in, grinning. *"Ay liz a bet a,"* she says with contagious enthusiasm. "I have a surprise."

A surprise? For me?

"Next Wednesday," she says. "I'm taking you to Arrinon for a bath."

Ah, the indulgence of a true, lavish bath! You're taking me to Arrinon? A bath! How wonderful.

That evening I write in my journal, breathing in the pungent scent of burning pine. Christmas is next month, and I already miss being with my family. Even though I've lived out of state for close to a decade, I've returned home for all but one Christmas. Now that I'm a million miles away, I appreciate my family's loving rituals: my mom waving at the window every day when my dad leaves for work; the family getting up early in the morning to wash our faces with dew on May Day; saying "rabbit rabbit" the first day of every month. Since my grandmother is quite old, and my dad's health is poor, either one could pass at any time. I miss my family, and the idea of a bath cheers me.

Finally, the bath day arrives. I'm ecstatic, picturing the steamy water up to my neck, my body lathered with silk bath oil and bubbles, my head just above the water line; candles lining the tub, gentle harps playing on the stereo as I slip deeper into the bath water. Our little tin car jolts past the vineyards, bare stalks during winter, and I feel a rich source of power like a fountain of grace rising within me. I am so, so grateful anticipating a long, hot bath.

Sean and Susan, a British couple I've met several times, welcome Camilla and me into their bare, stone apartment. I note a slight smell of mildew. There is just one small table and four hard chairs. We all kiss each other's cheeks, exchange pleasantries, and sit in the chairs which scrape against their floor. "Would you like to take a bath?" Sean asks at last.

I try not to act overeager, not to shout "Yes! Yes! Oh my God, I can't wait! Yes!"

"Yes, please," I say, my hands folded together neatly in my lap.

"Okay," he says. "But the water is *very* expensive. *Very* expensive."

Mmm. I think. How am I supposed to interpret that?

"Come," he says, taking me to a tiny bathroom, plastered with ceramic tiles, once white, now grey. While two walls of the bathtub/shower reach up the wall, the other two sides are only six inches high, up to my ankles. A hose and nozzle hang off the shower wall. "Use only one or two inches of water," Sean says. "Water is really expensive here," he repeats once more. "*Très, très cher*. Very, very expensive." His eyes pin me with distaste. These Brits don't like Americans any more than the French. I get the impression that this is a huge favor to Camilla, that he thinks little of me, and even less of my using his precious water.

I click the bathroom door shut and check out the dingy "bathtub," or so he called it—the short box into which I can barely squeeze to sit. His words, "*Très cher, très cher*," echo in my head.

Shit. There's no point in taking a bath at all. It's so tiny, and I'll be using their precious water. I unbutton my blouse, unzip my jeans, turn on the water, and listen to it dribble into the "tub." I wrap a towel around myself as the water heats up. Gingerly, I extend my toe, my foot, then squeeze the rest of my body into the "tub." I lift the hose, and a quiet whish of water sprays my body and hair. It never gets hot and steamy. When the water reaches my ankles, about to overflow, I turn it off. It drip, drip, drips down the wall until I turn the faucet tighter. Within minutes, the water feels icy. Enough! I stand, dry off, and pull the plug. The water gurgles down the drain.

From the peak of excitement to the valley of disappointment, how easily one can fall. I can't imagine a more miserable bath. I'm so bitter, even though I *know* Camilla was trying to be kind. Back in the stark living room,

Camilla jumps up from her seat, her tortoise shell glasses bobbing on her nose. "How was it?" she asks.

"*Ah,*" I say, faking a smile. "*Merci. Très Bien. Merci,*" speaking with as much grace as I can muster. Thank you. It was great! Just great. Thank you!

That was the end of my dreams about baths.

A few days later, Jean and Marian arrive for dinner. Randy hides in his room, preferring his solitude to strangers as usual. It's freezing cold, though. No one can stay away from the fire too long. Randy returns to the far edge of the table with his stamps and notebook. He touches the texture of the stamps from all over the world, and organizes them in their notebooks according to colors and designs.

"Stamp collecting is *rilly* quite popular," he tells me. "John Lennon collected stamps. So did Queen Elizabeth II, and Franklin Roosevelt. I heard there are twenty million stamp collectors in America."

I'm dumbfounded. "See?" He lifts his catalogues and leafs through the pages. "Collectors purchase these large catalogues to identify stamps and figure out their value. There are hundreds of them, from all different countries and time periods. I only have three."

Jean presents Camilla a small soft package wrapped in brown paper. Jean and Jacques drink in the *salle à manger* , while Randy sorts his stamps. Camilla, Marian, and I go to the kitchen to prepare supper. "*Bonjour, Ay liz a bet a. Tu vas bien?*" Marian asks. I'm always "*tu,*" not "*vous,*" to Marian; always a friend, not a stranger. Her grey eyes hint of blue like the sky at twilight. She's dressed in a hand-knit grey wool sweater, and her shoulders protrude like sticks in the style sought by fashion designers. Once again, I'm awed by the beauty of French women, even though Marian wears the same old sweater she wears every day. We all wear the same clothes, all the time—clothes that are the warmest and comfiest. For me, it's jeans and one of Jacques' old, blue-and-black, hand-knit wool sweaters.

At dinner, Camilla serves a small platter of brown, round lumps. "*Qu'est-ce que c'est?* What's that?" asks Louis.

Camilla beams. "Birds. Jean caught them. Such a delicacy!" Ah. The package Jean handed to Camilla.

Randy's cheeks narrow, his nostrils flare. "That's awful," he spits under his breath to me. "Serving birds!" Randy's face flushes, and he shoves the birds away, tearing some bread that he lathers with butter. He'll never eat a bird.

I serve myself a small pile, try a bite and, honestly, find they're not that bad. But Randy fumes at eating these tiny creatures. Randy's like a bird himself with his delicate manners, his thin bones, his quiet way of moving. No, he'll never eat a bird.

When we clear the plates, he bangs them on the kitchen table. "The Fontaines infuriate me!" he says. "They take their goats out in a bloody snow storm and they go and eat those helpless birds! What are they doing running a goat farm?"

"God, Randy! I can't stand your criticizing them all the time." I squirt dish soap into the basin and dunk the plates. We hear Marian and Jean, Camilla and Jacques, laughing in the other room. "That's all you do, Randy!" I say. "Rag! Rag! Rag! You're so negative all the time!"

"Well, you would be too if you knew what was going on!" Randy dries the plates with such vigor I'm afraid they'll break. By now I'm furious at him, but I also recognize the irony of my being so intolerant of his intolerance.

We're still growling at one another when Camilla comes in. *"Randy et Ay liz a beta,"* she says, "Go *doh29hs dh.*"

Randy and I glance at each other, questioning. We hear the twigs crackle in the fire. *"Qu'est-ce que c'est?"* I ask. "What?"

"*Go doh29hs dh.*" She scowls, irked at having to repeat herself. We dry our hands, put on our coats, and step outside into the night. When the door closes behind us, we both halt.

"What did she ask?"

"I haven't a clue."

We take in our surroundings: a shovel leans against the stone house, a stack of buckets lie in the dirt, chickens squawk in the shed. Randy raises his eyebrow. My mouth begins to quiver and we both burst out laughing. We have no idea what in the world she asked us to do.

"Buckets. Think we're supposed to fetch something?" The stars flicker in the midnight-black sky.

"Like what?"

Our argument becomes history, as we try to figure out our instructions. Deciphering puzzles is part of the allure of living with the Fontaines. The fun of being with Randy counteracts the wretched weather, the beastly chores, and the grim moodiness of Camilla. Except when it doesn't.

"Shall we try the chicken coop?" Randy asks. "Maybe we're supposed to collect eggs." Our feet crunch on the frozen mud as we head to the shed, which stinks of the chicken manure. My only experience with chickens and eggs was, again, at the Eastern States Exposition, the New England version of a Midwest county fair. My mom bought me sticky pink cotton candy, spun on a cardboard tube, before we explored the barn with chickens sitting on their eggs in their tidy coops. Each chicken had its own spot where the mama neatly laid her eggs, or so it seemed to me. I, now, follow Randy into the shed where he checks nooks and corners and lifts piles of hay. "Ahh," he said. "Here are a couple of eggs."

"You mean, chickens lay their eggs all over the coop?" I ask, stunned.

"What?" he asks in that sweet Aussie accent. "You think they lay them in little cardboard boxes for the market?" He snickers, shaking his head while I adjust my thinking.

"Well, I didn't think they'd be all over the place!" Eggs are buried in the prickly hay, on shit-covered shelves, in corners, outside in the mud. We search the coop and the surrounding chicken yard, and one by one, we roll as many eggs as we can in our shirts and return to the kitchen with our collection. Camilla stares, mouth half open, and starts to say something, but just takes the eggs and puts them in a yellow, plastic egg container. Her surprised expression says it all: we missed the boat. Oh, well. At least, Randy and I are buddies again.

Here on the farm, my mood soars and drops like a geyser, settling for a few days. When I read my book, or write in my journal next to Randy on the hearth, the fire crackling behind us, I feel like I'm in a magical place and time. I'm as happy and content as I've ever been. This night, I read *The Plague*, by Albert Camus, which I didn't like at first, but now, I'm completely absorbed in it.

Jacques, Marian, and Jean toss their hands in lively conversation, Jacques continually refilling the wine glasses. Camilla joins them after placing the rice pudding in the oven. I set down my book, and pour myself some wine, hoping to join in, but the French conversation moves at lightning speed, and I can't comprehend a word. Oh, well. My friend in Paris said following the dinner conversation is the last step in fluency. I've got a way to go.

I slide back down to the end of the table, where Randy fiddles with his stamps. I finish *The Plague,* picturing the hero who leans out his window and watches day after day, as people die. A review says the book "emphasizes the lack of control we have over our own lives."

Do we ever have control over our lives, I wonder, or are we just programmed by our genes and parenting? Can we actually make fundamental changes in our lives? Do all questions of human behavior come down to nature versus nurture? I love to wonder about Jung's concept of the collective unconscious. If the unconscious, something deeply embedded in us, catalyzes all our actions, how can we change? How can we ever let go of bad habits, like overeating or obsessing on a lover? Can we ever become the person we truly want to be?

My journal packs more questions than answers. Even so, *The Plague* is now my favorite book. Camilla serves the rice pudding, and as I chew a spoonful of raisins, I think about the protagonist who, facing the horror of a child dying, lets it strengthen his faith. This confuses me. But, when someone admits in the book, "I want to be a saint," it strikes a chord. What else is there, I think, after we have lost everything we loved, than to be a saint? When life seems like agony, faith carries people through the storm.

Perhaps, I muse, the most we can do in life is refrain from harming one another.

Chapter Nine

Death

"Ay liz a bet a." Michel greets me in the barn at the end of the day. His eyes are bloodshot, and he whips his hands around exclaiming something, something important. Someone is "*est tué*." Dead. Not just dead. Killed. Who? Who?

The mysterious Michel, who flits in and out of our lives so unexpectedly, repeats the same words over and over, the veins bursting on his shiny forehead. Not any of us…Camilla or Jacques or Randy or Louis or Marie or Marian or Jean? No.

Who?

Back at the house, the whole family—Camilla, Marie, Louis, Randy, and Jacques—lean on the table, listening to the radio. *Here Comes the Sun* plays in delicious English. The smoke from the fire permeates like incense. The radio announcer speaks. I turn to Michel, my heart pounding. "John Lennon?" I whisper. "John Lennon is dead?"

"*Oui*," he nods, lowering his head.

At last Michel has a friend, someone here in his home, who grieves as deeply as he. John Lennon is dead. *Imagine, I Want to Hold Your Hand, Octopus's Garden*—the radio plays on and on all night. The whole family is glued to the hard benches, listening, but Randy and I understand few of the DJ's words.

John Lennon marked milestones for my generation. In fourth grade, I sat cross-legged in our living room, watching the Beatles American debut on the Ed Sullivan show. I screamed like the bopper girls in the audience, shouting and singing, *I Want to Hold Your Hand!* The next Halloween, I dressed as Paul with a black suit and mop haircut.

I bought my first Beatles album, *The Beatles' Second Album,* in fifth grade, received *Rubber Soul* in sixth grade, and by eighth grade, the Beatles had moved onto psychedelics—not that I understood any of that. My friends and I sat on Amy's bed reading and re-reading the lyrics to *Lucy in the Sky* on the back of *Sergeant Pepper.* And by senior year at Northfield Mount Hermon, our religion teacher played *Imagine* over and over as we created abstract art projects.

We, the generation born in the fifties, schooled in the sixties, marked our lives with Beatles' albums, followed them (in spirit, at least) to India to see the Marahashee. Shocked by their breakup, we watched John and Yoko at their "Bed In" in Montreal. John and Yoko—getting together, separating, living in upstate New York, baking bread from scratch. I never considered John to be a figurehead, but now, abruptly, I realize he is—was—the icon of our generation. He lived on the edge, and he screwed up, and he got it together. He wrote and sang words that led so many of us to think about alternatives. Life could be more than getting married, getting a job, and raising kids. And now he's dead. Can it be true? The knot in my stomach rises up to my throat, choking me.

"What happened?" I ask.

"Some fool shot him," Jacques says. "There are lots of fools, especially in America." Jacques' words sting. I feel a mixture of shame and pride, a mixture of not wanting to be associated with America, yet also, appreciating my country's ideals. After all, John Lennon chose to live in America.

We listen to the radio and the sizzle of the fire. Michel and I have true communion that night. Our hearts mesh in a way no one else can understand.

John Lennon is dead, and Ronald Reagan is going to be president. My eyes are like wells of tears, overflowing, bottomless wells.

I've always liked reading. I come from a family of readers. Here on the farm, though, with so few distractions compared to life in the city, I concentrate more. I become fully absorbed in my books. The weather improves, for a day or two, and I read outdoors again. I'm riveted by Jerry Kozinski's *The Painted Bird,* his story about a child's escape from Eastern Europe during World War II. I'm convinced it's an autobiography, and am amazed to find it's fiction.

"Hi," Randy says.

I snap out of reading about the horror of Nazi Germany. "Randy, what are you doing here?" I regard my goats. Is everyone here? Grand Marnier's chewing leaves from the larger tree near Randy, and Elusive is eating from a fallen branch. "Hi," I say, feeling guilty, slipping my bookmark between the pages. "How's your day off?"

We chat for a few minutes. He scans the goats and asks, "Where's Coconut? I don't see Maurice." I scan the hillside. "*Allez!*" I call. "Coconut!" Randy hikes over the crest, calling, too. If he weren't here, I'd ask Frippo to round up our missing truants, but now, no way.

Coconut ambles into view, but no Maurice. And no Chinny. We return the rest of the herd to the barn, where Maurice waits, still as a statue, but no Chinny. We eat supper, and check the barn again. Still no sign of our missing goat. Oh, no. I need to go back up in the hills this dark, dark night.

Jacques hands me a flashlight. "Watch out for the wild boars," he says. He spreads his arms and butts his head to show how aggressive they are. I roll my eyes. Double shit. The trouble I get into for reading on the hills.

"I'll come with you," Randy says.

"Oh, no. You don't need to. I was the one herding." Inside, I'm saying *yes, please, please come!*

We bundle into our warmest coats, hats, scarves, and gloves and hike into the moonless night where silver stars dot the sky. Now, I'm really worried about boars. Jacques never warned me about anything before. What on earth would I do if I ran into one?

Randy and I climb the jagged rocks using our hands to brace ourselves, scrambling higher until we reach the crest. We turn off our flashlights. The night is mystical up here, with acres of empty black land stretching before us—

without a single sign of humanity—no power lines, no lights, no vehicles. Above us, a million stars, white like flakes of snow. We hear a faint ring. Silence. Another tinkle. The air smells so clean it seems alive. I feel my connection to the stars and the earth and the sky—and to Randy. Energy pulsates between us. We stand inches apart. He calls, "*Allez, allez!*" My breathing is shallow, as I reach out my hand, my pulse firing through my body.

Clap! Clap! Clap! The trance breaks with clapping hooves, growing louder on the rocks, and closer, until Chinny's outline comes into view. I drop my arm, my hand that Randy never saw or felt, and inhale the mounds of thyme that surround us.

"Chinny!" I say. We head for home.

Will Randy and I ever touch, or will we always orbit around each other at a safe distance? That is our mystery.

With Christmas just weeks away, I reflect on my family traditions: tree, dinner, presents, women in the kitchen, men drunk, me gorging. At the end of each Christmas day, my dad shooed my aunts, his sisters, out the door. He called them "insufferable" when they honked the car horn to say good-bye instead of blinking the car lights, as civilized people are supposed to do.

I write my mom and dad, saying that I want to be home for Christmas, but I'm in the middle of something I need to finish. Because it's hard to explain at this point, I don't say: *I'm on a quest to learn to believe in myself.* If I must be away, there's no place I'd rather be than here, in Languedoc with the Fontaines.

Yet, as soon as I let myself feel content, I think of Garner. I picture my tiny home in Eugene, and the DJ saying, "Okay, this is KZEL and its three P.M." Pause. The DJ comes on again. "Oh, wait a minute, its three-ten. No, three-fifteen. Oh well, whatever."

Garner cracked up. "That's Eugene for you. What time is it? Oh, well, whatever." He noticed things like that. It's true: "What time is it? Whatever." summed up Eugene. What will it take to exorcize Garner from my mind?

Once again, I yearn for someone like Susannah to talk with. Marian. If only I could talk to Marian. Last night, when she sipped her wine and spoke in a tongue I barely understood, Marian and Camilla seemed so close—like they were telling stories, sharing secrets. But between the accent and rapid speech, I didn't understand a thing.

Brilliant sunshine melts ice into mud, creating waterfalls along the hillside. On this spring-like day, a week after John Lennon died, I unlatch the barn door and Jacques says, "Leave Baby here."

"D'accord." Of course. Nothing unusual about leaving a goat behind once in awhile for hoof trimming. Yesterday, when I collected nuts for Baby, she stretched her head high like a giraffe, big and proud, although she barely reached my knees. She nuzzled her soft wet nose into my hand.

On this magnificent morning, I trot up the slope, feeling light with the change in weather, this warm spell under the blue sky. There's no better place on earth, I think, than these glorious days when the sun glows over the mountains.

At noon, I usher the goats back to their stalls, feeling a sense of joy. The warmth is welcome.

Something's off-kilter, though. "Randy," I say, as I sniff the cheese soufflé in the oven. "Baby wasn't in the barn when I brought the goats home."

At first Randy doesn't glance up from the *fromage de chevre* cup he's washing. Finally, he taps it down on the table. "Randy?" I ask, still touched by the glorious day. "What's up?"

He doesn't smile. "Randy." I speak slowly and distinctly. "What happened?" Randy hesitates. A log in the wood stove drops, banging against the door. I brace myself.

"They sold Baby," Randy says. "For someone's Christmas dinner."

A moment passes before it registers. Baby! My Baby!

I sprint up two rungs at a time and flop on my mattress. Baby is the first goat I truly loved. My *enfant.* I picture beckoning my little fellow so he'd huddle by my knees, and curl next to me; his little tongue tickling when he ate leaves from my hand. It can't be true. But, of course it is. Baby will be slaughtered for someone's Christmas dinner.

Day after day, Marie greets Ma Rosa after herding. "Ah, Ma Rosa," she says, stroking the orange nose, "Look at what I've got for you." She hands her oats and hugs the beast as much as you can hug a huge cow. "I love you, Ma Rosa." I leave the two lovebirds in the barn, still crushed by Baby's death and resentful about Ma Rosa's breaking my toe. Louis whizzes by. "Is Ma Rosa in the barn?"

"Yes, and," I mutter, "I'm back, too. And my toe is still purple and broken from the time that horrid bovine stomped on it!" But Louis is gone.

Randy and I set the table, the scent of peppery leek soup lingering in the air. "You know what gets me," I use one of Randy's favorite phrases, "is how much everyone looovvves Ma Rosa. She is so obstinate!" I slam the fork down so hard on the table it bounces. We laugh. "I mean, what's with them? Why, oh why, do they adore her so? Just because she's pregnant?"

In mid-December, Jacques announces that Ma Rosa will stay in the field near the barn rather than go out with the herd, since her baby is due any day now. Hallelujah! "You're going to be a Mama," Marie says in adoration as Ma Rosa's tummy balloons. I scoff. But, after witnessing days of Marie and Louis with Ma Rosa, my crusty shell begins to soften.

"I guess you're not too bad," I say the next afternoon. "Well, it's hard to hate a mama-to-be. I suppose I can feed you a little." I hand her a fist full of hay. "I don't forgive you for breaking my toe, but since you're going to have a baby, I'll let it go." I quickly add, "For now, that is. Until you have your baby."

"We'll take turns sleeping in the barn," Camilla announces, "until Ma Rosa delivers." The next morning at breakfast, after Marie and Louis' night in the barn, they tell us the obvious, "*Non.*" No calf.

For my night in the barn, I dress in my usual sleep clothes—thermal underwear, turtleneck, and sweater. I gather my coats, blanket, pillow, and an old flannel sleeping bag and meet Randy in the kitchen. With his arms overflowing with his piles of sleep gear, he grabs a flashlight, or "torch," as they call it in Australia, and we head to the barn. Cassiopeia and the Big Dipper glow like glitter against the night sky.

Jacques rearranges the rope partitions so Ma Rosa has ample space. Randy and I unroll our sleeping bags a few feet away from the cow and from each other. "Randy! I feel like I'm in a storybook, sleeping in a barn like this. Do you think she'll be born tonight?"

"Maybe," he says in his uninflected voice, his lips pursed like Ebenezer Scrooge. But, with the quiet bells in the cool air, a snort here, and a tail swish there, he relaxes.

"Hey, Randy, what do you think you're going to do when you leave here? When you go home?" Moonlight filters through seams in the barn's wall, onto his narrow cheeks, as he looks up toward the ceiling, his hands behind his head, elbows splayed.

"When I go home," he says. "I'll buy a caravan to keep behind my father's house."

"Caravan?"

"You know, the long metal homes that can sometimes be moved. But, mine will be tied down."

"Oh, mobile home." Ma Rosa rustles the straw covering the manure, and whacks the wall as she rearranges herself, then settles down.

"And what are you going to do with the caravan?"

"Well, when you open the front door, you'll see my stamp collection, all arranged in three glass cases on the wall."

"Mmm." I say, thinking once again that Randy resembles a British gentleman more than a teenage boy.

"There will be an aviary in front of the caravan with blue budgies and white rabbits."

"Budgies?"

"Oh, you know. The small, blue bird. Very peaceful."

"So, it will be like a giant cage with birds and bunnies?" I ask. At home I'd be snorting, full of sarcasm. Not here. I appreciate Randy's sincerity and love for beauty, animals, and birds.

"It will be lovely," he says, "a large enclosure with perches for the budgies and plenty of room for the white rabbits to run freely."

I try to picture the blue birds, the white bunnies, and the acres of fields for the sheep in the background. "Is that what you've been sketching in your notebook? Your aviary?" A moment of quiet, and I jump. "Randy! What's that? Is Ma Rosa going to have her baby? I hear something."

"No, not tonight I don't think."

"Randy, have you ever slept in a barn before?"

"No." A sheep baas from the end of the barn.

"I feel like Mary waiting for Jesus to be born. I can't believe we're sleeping on straw in a barn."

"Well, we are."

"I'm pretty comfy. Aren't you?"

"Yep."

We mash the hay, forming our nests, and try to sleep.

"Goodnight."

I lie awake, listening to several goats coo.

"So, Randy," I speak into the darkness. "What do you think about Christmas?"

He doesn't speak for several minutes. I smell the musky aroma of the barn. "Well, you know, my mum and I moved out from my dad's in spring. Then I came to live with Mum's friend, here in France. And now, I really should be home with Mum for Christmas. That's why I'm not having such a good time here."

So that's why he's been so grumpy, so irritable, so annoying.

"I can't decide whether to go to my mum's or my dad's when I leave here," he says, although he's clearly devoted to his mother. As we drift to sleep a second time, I feel a new wave of warmth toward Randy. We lie in the dark, silent, eighteen inches apart. My sexual feelings rise, and I resist them. Yes, I feel frisky after my months of celibacy, but Randy is immature, angry, and afraid. Together, we are so right; and we are so wrong. How easy it would be to reach out, to touch, but he'd flinch; I'm sure of it.

Ma Rosa doesn't calve. The next morning her tummy bulges further as she plods slowly outside the barn. We dote on the mama-to-be with pats, hugs, and extra hay. At three in the morning, two nights later, when rain drums on the eaves above our heads, Michel shouts from the kitchen, "Ma Rosa. *Le bébé!*" One by one, we hurl ourselves down the ladders, stuff our feet in our boots, and shoot to the barn where Ma Rosa lies like a beached whale, worn, tired, and proud.

Her baby, the size of a Great Dane, peers at the world with enormous saucer eyes and a tiny head, the size of a goat's. He's all wet, lying on a pile of straw, as darling as can be. In the lantern's yellow glow, he epitomizes innocence. He cocks his head, confused, lifts his sweet but slimy body, and walks a few steps. He stumbles, falls, tries again, and falls again. His mom pokes him with her giant nose. A few more wobbly steps, and we cheer, entranced by the newest member of the family.

A few days after the calf's birth, winter break from school begins. Marie and three friends from Toulouse drink alcoholic *cidre* in the *salle à manger*, blasting my Allman Brothers *Eat a Peach* tape, while I sweep the kitchen floor with a straw broom. I grit my teeth while they party and laugh at jokes I hear but cannot understand. I slam the stew pot on the table, seething with resentment, feeling like Cinderella.

A strapping boy with dark eyes and a flock of curls saunters into the kitchen. In barely understandable English he asks, "Hey, would you like some cider?"

"*Bien sûr,*" I say. I dry the pot, lay down my towel, and untie my apron. One of the boys, with dark green eyes the color of fir and a cleft chin, speaks a few words of English. He pours me a glass, raises it and says *"Salut."* We clink glasses and converse as best we can. He likes the opportunity to try out his English which is, in fact, better than my French. He's French, speaking English; and I'm English, speaking French, and we're having fun. Eventually, they leave to go horseback riding, and I return to my chores, upbeat after our little party.

In the barn Ma Rosa's baby teeters on his toothpick legs, balancing his gangly body, then cuddles next to his mom to stay warm. The frigid winds are back. How cold is it? Ten below? Twenty?

"Now," Camilla says, "*Ay liz a bet a,* no more using *la toilette.* We need to go pee pee outside." The frozen, half-barrel of shit will be too heavy to carry and dump.

When I herd, Grand Marnier and Elusive poke their damp noses into my pockets, hoping for nuts, while I read *Anna Karenina* with my gloved fingers. After giving up on hope for love, Levin and Kitty reconnect and marry. When they each write their initials in dust on the table, I imagine myself writing like Tolstoy. Of course, Garner's face flashes before me—that smooth white skin, his teeth ever so slightly overlapped, those alluring eyes smiling at me. Surely, the way to get over a man is not to isolate oneself on a goat farm in the mountains of Languedoc.

Anna Karenina consumes my time and concentration until the sky darkens, and hail suddenly strikes like shards of glass. I tuck my book in my pack, pull up my hood, and my herd and I dash for the cover near a *petit* oak. When the hail lightens, I need to entertain myself. First, I recite the St. Francis of Assisi prayer I memorized in my first weeks on the farm: *Lord, make me an instrument of thy peace*… When the air clears, I pace in what the Buddhists monks call a walking meditation: slow steps, hands together, trying to "listen to God." Spirit, God, Belief—they all fuse together here in nature.

"Okay, Lucy," I say as the goat wiggles next to my knees. "What should I do next?" I feel so free, like a ten year old making up games. I close my eyes, pretending I'm blindfolded, and wander aimlessly, trying to visualize the warm orange flames in the fireplace. Playing these goofy games is one of my best survival techniques up here in the winter storms.

So, what am I going to do when I leave the farm, I ask myself?

"*Allez, allez,*" I call to my tribe as we traipse to a new spot. Morocco's not that far, and I've never traveled to a non-Christian country. Spain sounds exciting, too, but so does the art in Italy, and of course, my friend Fred is in Germany. Oh, and I must see the mountains of Switzerland. Maybe it will be months before I leave, but right now, I like the sound of hot sun. Morocco. Yes, Morocco is calling.

Chapter Ten

The Fête

"Tomorrow," Camilla tells me, "we're having a. *fête.*" A party to celebrate the winter solstice. What first began as a spiritual holiday for the pagans eventually led to Christmas. I'm excited, not so much for the Solstice/Christmas party, but for staying indoors, out of the sleet and snow.

The five Fontaines, Marian and Jean, the British couple of the famed bath, and Randy and I spruce up in our cleanest jeans and prettiest sweaters. Jacques dresses in a shirt without holes. Marie sets out fine bone china adorned with pink roses. Where did that come from? I can't believe they have that gorgeous china burrowed in the bureau in this sparse *salle à manger* .

Camilla flits about, pulling cakes from the oven, basting the roast pig, and tending the potatoes over the fire. Exquisite aromas of wine, pork, and thyme mingle through the house.

We all gather at the table, first choosing between *Muscat,* a sweet wine derived from one of the oldest domesticated grapes, and *Pastis*, an anise-flavored aperitif similar to absinthe, but bottled with sugar. Those who drink the *pastis*—about forty-five percent alcohol—quickly become animated. It's delicious. Jacques lifts his glass in a toast. "*Bon santé,*" he says.

We raise our glasses in response. "*À la vôtre!*" Like American Thanksgivings, *fêtes* center on food, family, friends, and drink. Mostly food and drink. But whereas Americans tend to dive into their meals like gluttons, the French savor each bite, each word of conversation.

Camilla begins by passing black olives the size of small plums, rich and succulent, fresh from Andorra. Every three months or so, Camilla and Marian head out before the sun rises to the tiny mountain country of Andorra, situated in the Eastern Pyrenees between Spain and France. They return home late at night with bags and boxes of food and other goodies. At the *fête,* the olives circle the table a second time, along with more *pastis* and *Muscat.* I never liked olives, until these. They melt in my mouth—sweet, tangy, delectable.

Jacques and Jean chatter, and Camilla jumps in, even more vibrant than usual. Laughter flows with the wines. Marian sits tall, quiet, with her sandy blond hair dry, almost wiry, framing her lovely face. The next course is *hors d'oeuvres* of fresh meats: liver pate, sliced sausage, and sliced ham. My sausage tastes slightly salty, a rich flavor seasoned with fresh herbs from the hills. Red wine replaces the *Muscat* and *pastis.* An hour flies by.

Next, Camilla serves salad. Randy, in his quiet manner, adds wood to the fire, while I try, in vain, to catch a few words of the conversation. Although Marian is expressionless, the rest of the crowd tells stories, waving their arms in the manner of the French, joking, laughing, and drinking more wine. Marian smiles appropriately at jokes, but has a dreamy air about her, as though in a different world.

Camilla serves the main course: roasted pig. Its charred head looks alive. I block my eyes with my hand. No sirree. No pig's head for me. Jacques slices the fragrant meat. Camilla adds herbed potatoes, and once again, plates go around the table. Maybe I can't look at the animal's head, but my, how I can eat the rest of it. I've never tasted anything as luscious as this neighbor's swine, garnished with our home-grown vegetables, doused in buttered herbs from the hillside.

Each bite graces our taste buds like a gift from the gods, and still, the wine flows. I begin to get giddy, giggling while Randy becomes more and more remote. He doesn't like people to start with. Drunken people, he detests. Both Louis and Marie drink wine, too. They bounce on the bench, trying to squeeze a word into the adult's conversation. With Randy's back rim-rod straight, he probably hopes the *fête* will end soon. It will not. Another two hours pass, and now, on to the cakes.

Camilla relishes the role of hostess. Dressed in a new green sweater with shiny silver earrings, she is radiant. Her face glows, her smile fills the room, and she is in her element. This, it seems, is her reward for working so hard—entertaining family and friends. The dutiful, slave-driving, head of house has disappeared, replaced by an ebullient social butterfly. Quiet Jacques has transformed into a gregarious partier, joking, carrying on. Camilla and Jacques are now a fun-loving couple, having the time of their lives.

And Marian! Marian finally joins in, speaking, laughing, waving her hands. Oh, how I marvel at Marian—her confidence, her composure, her grace.

Marie, Randy, and I clear the dishes and bring in three cakes from the kitchen: a chocolate, apple, and a yellow cake. As we digest our final bites, burps pop throughout the room and belts are loosened. Camilla returns with coffee-chicory and Grand Marnier, the sweet liqueur.

Randy whispers to me, "We need to go feed the goats. They'll be starving." I survey the laughing faces—even Marian beams—and I wish I understood more of the conversation. Reluctantly, I place my fork on the table. Randy and I excuse ourselves with an "*a toute à l'heure*" and a "*merci.*" Gotta go.

Once outside, I spread out my arms and twirl under the vast sky, red and lilac and grey where the first star peeks over the mountains. Yes, it will be fine to stay here through this wretched winter. In my drunken stupor, I help Randy add hay to the troughs, but the goats bombard us, each one trying to squeeze in front of the other. The larger goats knock over the smaller ones, clanging their bells as they charge to the food. Once the big ones eat, we cordon them off, so the little guys can have their fair share.

This freezing night, Marie and I snuggle close, two sisters trying to stay warm. I fall asleep smiling, reflecting on our *fête,* the reward for herding in these cruel, winter winds.

When I wake at sunrise, my head thunders like an air hammer. God, I forgot about hangovers. After breakfast, I gather a stack of clothes to mend, and hum in front the fire.

Marie tinks her spoon against her bowl of milk and says, "Randy and *Ay liz a bet a*, we need wood. Bring the wood in the house." Randy and I glance at each other and smirk. What is Marie doing giving us orders?

"I'm not going to cut that wood for you," I say, my shoulders squared.

"Do you want to leave the farm?" she asks in her saucy voice.

Red embers flicker on the hearth. "If you want me to leave because I am not going to cut your wood, then yes. I'll go in a heartbeat." By now I can communicate in sentences one on one. I almost scream, "Get off your bloody ass and get the wood yourself." But Marie turns back to her milk as though the conversation never happened, and I go back to my mending. Would I have stood up to Marie like that three months ago? Maybe. I know I've grown a notch.

As I thread the needle, I note Marie's exquisite beauty. In Eliot's *Adam Bede*, beauty leads to tragedy. What fate awaits Marie? Though only fourteen years old, Marie can pass for seventeen, if not twenty. I remember one time when we strolled together by a wooded road next the river. She wore a black coat of cheesy material, one of the ugliest coats I'd ever seen, with a flowing purple scarf around her neck. With her rose cheeks, demure smile, and auburn hair shining in the sunlight, she was angelic. Her beauty, despite that gruesome coat, surpassed fashion show models.

At evening supper, Marie and Louis argue, again. First she hits him, screams, and then Louis slugs her in retaliation. "Mama," Marie whines. Camilla's eyes narrow and dart between her two children. She yells back at Marie, taking Louis's side. "But, Mama," Marie snivels, pleading with her mother, wanting attention like a six-year-old. I want to say, "Marie, you're driving us crazy, quit acting like a little spoiled brat. Act your age and your mom might be nicer to you." We're all fuming at her at this point.

An hour later, when Randy and I are washing dishes, Marie asks in her purring voice to use my cassette player, and suddenly, I'm ready to forgive all her manipulating, screaming, and fussing. She's the type of woman I've only read about, who exudes such beauty that people around her overlook her flaws. "Sure," I say.

I'm feeling down, though, and barely notice when the phone rings. Randy and I are drying the pots when Jacques comes in, a dull look in his eyes. "A friend called," he says, "about a goat grazing in Gordona." Gordona is a couple of kilometers away. Crap, I think. Not good.

"Which goat do you think it is?" I ask Randy, when Jacques leaves the room. "How long has he been missing?"

"I haven't a clue."

Oh, this is horrible. What kind of goat herders are we? Losing a goat, and even worse, not even knowing it? Am I going to be fired after all? I've got to quit thinking that way.

An hour later, we hear the loud motor and put on our heavy coats to meet the truck in the drive. "It's Chinny," Randy says. Chinny jumps down, and Randy takes his collar, leading him to the barn. I find a pile of hay, feed him, and watch him eat. Randy says nothing.

We return to the house by the fire and I pick up my journal. I'm so depressed. My world isn't really caving in, but it feels like it is. My stomach and head both hurt.

Herding in the awful weather is wretched. I miss my family, and can't believe I won't be with them for Christmas. And how did we lose Chinny? Poor Chinny, overnight in all these storms. I write in my journal, but can't rid myself of these emotions. I'm at a new low, the lowest since arriving on the farm.

The next morning, I awake to whispers and giggles, and a sweet, buttery scent. I open my eyes as a tray slides across the floor from the ladder. Marie and Randy stick their heads up from the top rung, each with ear-to-ear grins.

I muster myself into a sitting position, careful not to bang my head on the rafters. "*Crêpes*! My favorite!" I say, tossing my hair off my face. "Thank you! Thank you!" They are so kind, I feel overwhelmed. They know me, they love me, and, best of all, they know *crêpes* will cheer me up.

Two days before Christmas, another storm! My troops and I plunge through snowflakes the size of dimes that plummet from the eerie, platinum sky. The flat light on the snow stretches miles, as far as my eyes can see, half-blinding me. I pull up my collar, trying to shield myself, and yank down my hat so low I can barely see. The goats stick to me, as though saying, what are we doing shivering out in this blasted blizzard?

At dinner, I rub my hands, trying to warm up. "We're going to separate Ma Rosa from her calf," Camilla says. Personally, I'd much rather stay by the fire. Instead, the whole family treks down to the barn, where Ma Rosa and her baby lie together. Camilla pulls the calf's collar, while the rest of us lift her to her feet and lead her to a secluded corner of the barn.

Ma Rosa doesn't like this one bit, and neither does her son. The restless goats shuffle the matted hay with their hooves, and Ma Rosa jerkily sweeps her head from side to side, ringing her giant bell as she stretches her neck, making an awful groan while trying to reach her baby. Jacques and Randy hold onto Ma Rosa's neck, using all their strength to restrain the giant unhappy mama.

On some level, Ma Rosa knows what I do not: that, as a result of this separation, the people will benefit first, with frothy cow's milk, a true delicacy over our boxed milk. We'll have fresh butter and cream to eat and sell. Yum! And then her baby will be sold and eaten as veal.

While we drag Ma Rosa's baby from her, I reflect on my separation from my own mother, an uneven journey. While thousands of miles divide us, her voice rings in my head. Is life, I wonder, about this journey in which we separate from our parents, and then transform, emerging as our true self? Is that what believing in ourselves is all about? Knowing our mothers are part of us, always with us, but they are not us? That we, in fact, are our own judges? When I think of mothers, I think of judgment. Is that the way it's supposed to be?

Two nights later, Marie beseeches Camilla with, "Mama, it's freezing out. *Le bébé* is used to cuddling with his mama. And now he's alone on the other side of the barn, so cold and lonely." The wind howls outside the door. "Please, Mama!" Marie says. "We need to bring him inside. Please!"

Camilla looks up while her hands quickly scrub, clean, and dry the dishes. "Alright! Go! Go get him!"

Ten minutes later, Baby Rosa clomp, clomp, clomps his little hooves on the cement in the *salle à manger,* still awkward on his feet. He patters his way around the table; around and around he goes, with Louis chasing the calf, and Marie yelling, running after Louis like a wild scene from Dr. Seuss. Clatter! Clatter! Clatter! Run, run, run! *Le bébé* draws his ears back, and his eyes grow to the size of soup bowls, frightened, as he circles the table again and again.

Jacques, the spoiler, shouts, *"Arête!* Everyone stop!" Silence. Embers hiss. "He'll trip and hurt his leg." I feel a bubble rise in my throat, giggles rising into hearty laughter when our newest child finally stops—a scared little thing away from his mama.

On Christmas Eve the sun reappears, casting a sheen on the puddles of melted ice. It's my day off, and Natasha, my canine buddy, and I explore the ruins across the street. Once again, I'm awed by the sense of holiness and enchantment which emanates from the hills.

"This is why I'm here, Natasha. To feel this sense of the sacred."

"No Christmas tree?" I ask, Marie, back at the house.

"What's that?" she asks. When I explain, Camilla scowls. Cut down a tree? Put it inside? Put a rope of twinkling lights around the branches, and then hang little balls that break when the dog wags his tail? Why would you ever do that?

At twilight under the lavender sky, Louis, Marie, and Randy squeeze into the backseat of our tiny truck, and I sit in front next to Camilla. Jacques nods goodbye as we adventure off. Christmas Eve begins at the home of an English family a few villages away. They greet us cheerfully in French, kisses all around, the home smelling of wax candles. Marie and Louis play with their children in the bedroom, while Randy and I try to follow the brisk, French conversation between Camilla and the Brits who pour glass after glass of wine, rarely speaking in English. Camilla, my sister, my friend, partner, and fellow reveler for the night, gesticulates like usual, chattering and laughing. Still, I miss half her words. What a difference between communicating one-to-one versus at a party like this.

"*Merci,*" Camilla says to the family as we prepare to leave. "*À toute à l'heure* ." We all kiss each others' cheeks, pour into the car, and *vite!* Off we go to the community-center-type place, where we danced to Eric Clapton a few months ago. Camilla guides us into the large, dank, but lively, room filled with long tables and fold-up chairs, all set up in rows. She purchases two LOTTO cards each for the children and Randy and me, and five for herself. They look like BINGO cards, except with only nine squares, three rows and three columns.

The air sizzles with enthusiastic gamblers packing the room. A fellow with a plump belly, unshaven face, and infectious smile of yellow teeth summons his pomp and bellows words Randy and I barely understand. He's probably listing the rules of the game. Fellow players, old and young, are wrapped in layers of sweaters and smile to one another with crooked teeth, lifting their markers, ready for action. From his spot at the head of the room, our leader roars out the numbers. "*Soixant nerf,*" he calls, "*soixant nerf.*" Randy and I glance at each other and repeat again and again (*soixant nerf, soixant nerf*), until one of us translates, "sixty-nine!" We immediately mark it on our card. In the meantime, Camilla bends her neck, nose almost touching her cards, and *dot, dot, dot,* she marks her cards, one after another.

None of us wins anything the first round. Time for the break. *Voila*, a refrigerator opens, and a gentleman with a bent back, in a tattered grey jacket, stacks bottles of beer on the table, ready for purchase. Camilla buys us all a round, and she, Randy, Louis, Marie, and I joke with each other, drinking the rich ale. Even Randy's smile, his small white teeth shining, seems genuine. After the break, the game begins anew. Randy and I again sit elbow to elbow, repeating *trente six, trente six,-ah! Thirty-six!* Again, none of us wins, but what might have been a boring game if we'd actually known our French numbers well, is great fun.

As the game winds down, Camilla whispers to us. "I have a good feeling." She pushes her glasses up her nose. "Concentrate on number thirty-nine." We all squeeze our eyes, trying to focus and concentrate: thirty-nine, thirty-nine thirty-nine. The room hushes, and the fire in the wood stove sputters, spitting small sparks. The announcer shouts, "thirty-nine!" We shoot out of our seats, clapping hysterically. Hurray! Camilla wins! And, win she does: two hams, a bottle of wine, sausage, canned pineapple, and a box of biscuits.

We cart Camilla's winnings to the car, laughing and shouting, and pile in for yet another stop. We arrive at a small, sparsely decorated house, scented with dried thyme. The thirty-something couple serves wine and fresh, almost bitter, cheese. A babbling Camilla expounds about LOTTO, her winning basket, the ham, the wine. She speaks so fast, I miss her exact words, but her enthusiasm conveys more than words. She's thrilled.

Visit over, now a few minutes before midnight, we drive to a small Catholic church. The mass here resembles the only Catholic mass I've ever attended, in the Berkshire Mountains with my friend Christine's family twenty years ago. A priest and three children stride up and down the aisles. Frankincense (or is it myrrh?) saturates the air as one child sways a metal ball of incense and another rings the bells. A few muffled coughs interrupt the twang of bells.

Then, what is *that?* The priest and the children stop before the oddest sight. What on earth is a miniature merry-go-round doing in a church? With dolls on it, no less? The priest moves forward, gesturing his hands in ritual. Is that French? Or Latin? I've studied both and can't recognize either. Foreign as this all is, I feel a reverential connection with my own version of God, the idea of Love, so different from the Catholic patriarch. The priest utters his sermon, serves a communion with wafers, which none of our crew eats, and concludes with a solemn organ and clarinet.

Ahhh. We're all tired, but amped. Now, Christmas!

On the way home, Marie says, "Randy and *Ay liz a bet a*, you're part of the family." It means so much to me. "You're part of the family." Why is this so important that I earn my way into their family? Randy could care less. Animals are his priority, not people, even if his cold attitude is only a personal defense. No one calls him on Christmas—not his mother, father, brother or sisters.

The children shout, *"Papa! Papa!"* as they rush through the kitchen door. "Look what Mama won!" It's now 1:30 in the morning. We exchange gifts in front of the glowing orange coals. Camilla gives me a stone box that resembles marble, topped with inlaid abalone. It's tiny, the size of an olive, and can be used to hold a pair of earrings. My mom sent *The Reivers* by William Faulkner. My only presents, but they mean so much.

A few days later, Jacques gives me a hand-stitched and hand-cut leather strip of bells. Oh, my word! These are gorgeous. "*Merci, Jacques.*" I feel unable to state my appreciation. Randy and I chipped in together to give Camilla and Jacques Chivas Royale that Randy bought during a visit to town with Camilla. I wish I'd thought of something more personal, but I didn't.

It's the middle of the night, two o'clock Christmas morning, and time for *hors d'oeuvres* and a huge dinner: fish, vegetables, and desserts that Camilla and I prepared earlier. You'd think we'd be stuffed after eating all evening, but we devour it all. Finally, bedtime. Three o'clock.

"*Bonne nuit,*" Randy and I say to everyone, our arms stuffed with pillows and blankets and the flashlight, torch. We're all taking turns sleeping in the barn near the precious baby calf, now the most valued member of the household. Together with the goats, the sheep, Ma Rosa, her baby and

Frippo and Natasha, Randy and I settle in to sleep—a proper distance between us, of course. Although our beds of straw are itchy, with sharp tips poking through the blankets, I'm thrilled to spend the night in a stable with baas and coos and big cow snorts—a perfect celebration on Christmas Eve.

Randy and I sleep until 10:00 o'clock. Back at the house, Camilla scurries through her cooking. "I just love to work," she says for the millionth time. "Not just work. Work done well and quickly." Yeah. I know. One of the most important lessons I've learned here is that "convenience" is a dirty word. If we work hard, we add quality to life—like the difference between McDonald's and a gourmet meal. Camilla loves her work, and that's rubbing off on me.

With the table set and food prepared, we wait for Jacques' family to arrive. And we wait. And wait. Randy adds more wood to the fire as Marie begins sparring with Louis. "I did not."

"You did, too!" Bop, bop, bop.

"Stop it!" Camilla intervenes.

We hear the car sputter up to the house and park. The kids leap up and run outside, shouting, "They're here, they're here!" Finally, long overdue, Jacques arrives with his parents, sister, and brother.

Jacques' brother's personality matches his stiff tie and black coat. Once a counselor, he majored in philosophy, and once herded goats, so he and I should get along well, right? I find him pretentious and arrogant. I don't like him one bit.

His sister, though, is a different story. At twenty-four, she studied philosophy for a year, and now works in a hospital. With her hair loosely coiffed, partially tied back, she moves gracefully like a French woman, just like Marian, the perfect balance between tension and relaxation, light-hearted, but intelligent, and truly a pleasure.

When the phone rings, Marie and Louis bound from their bench. "It's for you, *Ay liz a bet a!*" Marie and Louis squabble over who's going to hold the extra black earpiece to listen in. The fact they can't understand the conversation is inconsequential. My mom, dad, sister Susan, and her boyfriend, Josh, are on separate phone extensions at home.

Christmas at the Fontaines is wonderful, but it doesn't compare to hearing my family's voices. It's afternoon in Massachusetts, and they've come home from my older sister Joan's where, like every Christmas morning, they ate breakfast with her, her husband, son, and Nana, my grandmother. They'll all come to our house for Christmas dinner with my aunts. Tradition, tradition, year after year. For better, or for worse. For better, I decide. I return to the table for the last of dessert, a little homesick, a little tipsy, but mostly touched by this wonderful Christmas.

December 26, 1980. Another day off. I've been curious about an abandoned, stone sheep barn that I discovered once while herding. After a few wrong turns on the hillside, I elbow my way through the thorny bushes that block the entrance, and find a surprisingly clean, dirt-floored room with a single cross beam inches above my head. A few large rocks and ancient, broken pots are strewn about. It smells like fresh soil—no droppings, no urine smell, no evidence that other animals have plowed through the prickers. My refuge for the day.

I write in my journal. It's as though I were in a cocoon, a chrysalis, undergoing some fundamental change in my inner core. A metamorphosis. Both my mom and grandmother asked if I'm going to write a book while I'm here. Sure, I've written daily in my journal for ten years, but that's not writing a book. I've become more confident, but on the topic of writing, I'm still stuck.

"Who's going to guard the goats this morning?" Jacques asks the next day. Whoa! He's never asked us that before. That elevates Randy and me to a new status. Every other time, Jacques or Camilla always told us what to do, when to herd.

"I am," I answer.

"The goats can stay in the barn this afternoon," Camilla says at noon dinner, "because the storm is supposed to be particularly severe." Thank God the goats can remain in the barn. After dinner, Randy and I bundle up to feed our tribe. We try to dole out the hay fairly, but the larger ones push and shove, hustling around us, barring the little ones from their food.

The storm clears for a moment, and Jacques and I plunge through the snow mid-way up our calves to attach a battery, that looks like a car battery, to electrify the fence at a new paddy for the horses. Jacques' fingers nimbly tie the wires in the frigid air, while I hop from one foot to another, hands in my pocket, useless. Back at the house, cold and snow-soaked, Jacques announces, "Time to milk the cow," and he heads to the barn with a pail.

"Milk! Fresh milk!" Marie cries. After comforting and babying Ma Rosa for weeks, before and after she bore her calf, we'll finally drink cow's milk.

Ten minutes pass. A half hour. Finally, with gusts against Jacques back, the kitchen door bangs open, slamming the wall. Jacques tears off his snow-covered hat and shakes his head. No. No milk. The children groan.

"This is what gets me," Randy says to me in a low voice, as though someone can understand what he says. "Jacques doesn't know anything about milking cows. He thinks Ma Rosa doesn't have any milk, but she's just holding back for her baby."

Randy helps Jacques the following day, and they bring home a quarter of a pail, about a pint. We each get a small glass. It's so good! I've been drinking milk from a box since I landed on the farm, and I'm startled by how sweet and delicious the fresh milk tastes. Have I ever actually drunk fresh milk before? I have not.

"How'd the milking go?" I ask Randy.

"Not good." He shakes his blond locks. "Ma Rosa doesn't want to settle down, and Jacques makes it worse. At least we got this little bit." Within a week, Jacques has a giant black eye from a well-aimed kick, courtesy of Ma Rosa. Does he see a doctor? Does anyone? Ever? No, no, and no.

After supper on the night of the black eye, I chat with Jacques and Marie. Jacques disdains *"les choses modernes."* He tells me that the different regions of France—Languedoc, Provence, Bretagne, Normandy, and so forth—used to have their own customs, their own dress, language, songs, and dance. "And now that's disappearing." He sips his wine. "Today, everyone, everywhere, wears denim jeans. Levi's—now he's almost spitting—represent the loss of regional uniqueness. The loss of the unique cultures." You can be sure, we'll never catch Jacques in a pair of dungarees.

Buried in the bureau, near the fine bone China, is a large coffee-table book with photos of different Native American cultures, of teepees, feather head garb, and leather clothes. "I'd love to visit America," he says. "Go to the Apache and Hopi reservations. To the Blackfoot." These Native Americans who live, or lived, close to the land, and whose Great Spirit is found in nature—these are the cultures Jacques most admires.

Growing up on the East coast, I never encountered true Indians. I took a class called *American Indians* at Ohio Wesleyan. When I traveled across America, I saw reservations for the first time: ramshackle huts with outhouses and broken-down cars. I'd never seen such rural poverty. Somehow, I can't picture today's reservations on a tourist brochure.

The more Jacques speaks, the more I understand why he and Camilla are living out here in the mountains, snowstorm after snowstorm. I gather that, like so many Americans who migrated to Oregon in the sixties and seventies, the Fontaines, and most of their friends from Northern France, Germany, and England, came to Languedoc as part of the "back to nature" movement, seeking freedom in the mountains without the government harping on them.

"That makes sense," says Randy, who understands French more than I, although I speak it better than he. "With all the health regulations in America and Australia, you wouldn't be able to raise goats or sell the cheese and milk like the Fontaines do." Here, these hardy individualists can live off the land without interference.

Chapter Eleven

The New Year

On New Year's Eve, the cat births kittens in the barn. The moment her mama turns her back, Jacques scoops the kittens into a burlap sack, and comes back empty-handed a half-hour later. He's drowned the kittens in the creek. I love cats, I love kittens, and my throat feels like there's a melon caught in it, but still, I don't feel as badly as I would have in September. The balance of life and death continues. I'm getting a little more used to death every day.

For the rest of school vacation, Marie and Louis visit friends in other villages. Our mystery Michel, the oldest brother, disappears as well, leaving Randy and me, and Jacques and Camilla, like two friendly couples who celebrate New Year's Eve together. Five minutes before midnight, Camilla arranges a plate of *petit fours* from the *pâtisserie,* surprising us with a little party. Jacques pours the wine. Randy and I admire the treats, little square cakes with intricate green and yellows flowers of frosting. We each speak slowly and enunciate carefully, and *voila,* all four of us communicate. Soon, even Randy is laughing and joking. He's having fun! Jacques pours more wine. We nibble on the yummy sweets that only a French *pâtisserie* can create.

I'm struck by Camilla's effort in making the little party for just the four of us, the four of us who live with each other day after day, meal after meal. Certainly, we're worth it. Worth skipping "convenience," to have fun on New Year's Eve.

On New Year's morning, I awake to sounds of animals: the goats' bells ring, roosters crow, and Ma Rosa moos. No screaming, yelling, and crying children. Peace. None of Louis' and Marie's fighting that usually drives me crazy. Appreciating this quiet morning, I toast a slice of bread on a stick in the fireplace. "Would you like to go horseback riding?" Jacques asks.

I glance at Randy, and we both nod. "Sure!" I'm so serene by the fire, I forget the fact that I don't like to ride. I only like the *idea* of riding. Denial is such a powerful force. All I think is, *what a fun way to start 1981!*

Camilla and I wash the breakfast dishes, Jacques and Randy milk the cow, and I pump from the few goats who still have a tad of milk. When Camilla throws a blanket over the horses' flanks, a sense of dread shoots from my spine to my toes. I'm terrified I'll have to ride without a saddle. Jacques tosses the rope around my horse, Mistral, and I help with the bridle, and then, phew, a saddle.

We mount—Randy and I on leather saddles, Jacques and Camilla on plain blankets, all of us using ropes for reins. Our horses trot and gallop through the field, past the house, onto the road, and I feel like I belong in a western movie. "Head 'em out! Raaaawwwwhide," I sing to myself. It's exciting because it's New Year's morning, because we're horseback riding, and because it's the one and only time the four of us have done anything together without the children.

Mistral walks calmly, obeying my tugs on the rope reins. Jacques' horse, restless from the get go, neighs, rears his front legs, neighs again, and spins around. I try to avoid him, tightening Mistral's reins with my back tensing. Jacques finally trots ahead, while Camilla brings up the rear. I realize I've been holding my breath. Randy focuses on his reins, then looks ahead. He doesn't much like riding either.

We giddy-up, smelling the damp sage dotting the surrounding fields, and ride the five miles to Marian and Jean's tiny village of a few houses. The homes resemble ours, about one hundred years old, built of stone and mortar, with a couple of tiny windows. Jean emerges from his house, his hair and clothes as rumpled as usual. "*Bonjour! Entrez.*"

I guess he means, "Tie up your horses on the rail in front—like in the wild, wild West—and come on in." Jacques' horse spins around like a top, completely out control. He heaves his front legs high into the air, and Jacques yanks the rope reins. The horse—irrespective of common courtesy, unaware a horse belongs outside, not inside, swerves right into Jean's house. Jacques ducks under the entrance beam as his horse claps his hooves against the cement, and circles the living room. To make things worse, Mistral follows after him, with me barely holding on, laughing from the depths of my belly. We trot around the living room twice, before galloping out the front door, just in time for Jacques to duck once more. Mistral dashes after his buddy, and I quickly lower my head, nearly bopping it on the beams. Once outdoors again, Jacques and I both jump off our horses, tie them to the hitching post, straighten our faces, and walk in for tea, shoulders back, as though nothing odd happened at all.

The house smells of the mold that grows in damp, unheated rooms. Marian enters from the side, presumably from the kitchen, wearing what I've come to think of as her uniform: well-worn jeans and long grey sweater, pulled out of shape from daily wear. Her face is paler than usual, her blue eyes lifeless, almost as grey as her sweater, and her smile looks forced. She seems ghostlike, almost a wisp, as she sits beside Jean.

Neither of them offers us food or drink. The cold house is barren, except for a handmade, wooden handrail, polished until shiny, which leads to the loft. The walls are blank. The fireplace has no fire nor wood. We're all quiet for a few moments, then Camilla begins to speak. The conversation feels awkward, forced. They have no running water, electricity, telephone, or heat. The room is desolate. We soon say *à toute à l'heure*, see you later. We kiss on the cheeks, and ride back uneventfully.

As we gallop home, I wonder about Marian. Why was she so pale today, paler than usual? Her movements reminded me of a string-puppet, stiff, calculated, cautious. What was going on? Was she sick? I'd guess they rarely have visitors, given our cold reception.

I appreciate Camilla and Jacques' hard work even more than before. We always have wood, a fire burning, food, and drink for guests. We had a New Year's party, even though there were just four of us. How much more difficult life could be here in the frigid mountain winters without wood, without the source for water, without our animals.

"We're going to go to the parents," Camilla tells Randy and me, as we lead the horses back to their paddy. "For three days." Now, one might think they'd prepare us to run the farm for three days by ourselves, but, no. We look at each other, dumbfounded. "Okay," we say in unison.

Mmm, I think. With the children on vacation, and Michel who knows where, Randy and I will be alone for three days. Three days! Freedom, with the Fontaines gone! I want to raise hell. But, how do I raise hell on this isolated farm? With Randy? Randy—so good, so trustworthy, so responsible.

I herd in the afternoon. When the sun falls behind the mountains, the sky a misty purple, we need to milk Ma Rosa. My first time milking a cow. So far, milking her has not gone well for Jacques and Randy.

Randy attempts something new. He ties the cow's horns with a rope to a bar in the barn, and then tries to tie one leg. She kicks, leans forward, with her horns up and ears back, terrifying me. She kicks again. Over and over. Randy and I team together, out of the range of her violent hoof. With me squeezing the teats for milk, Randy holds the bucket steady and pats her head. At last, we get milk. A half a bucket in an hour. Not a speedy operation.

Back at the house, I pour myself some boxed milk, warm it on the stove, and add Grand Marnier. "You know," Randy says, climbing the ladder to his loft, "I'm wondering if we can figure out another way to feed the goats in the barn on stormy days." He pauses, thinking. "We lose a lot of hay carrying it, and the little ones never get their fair share." I hear his footsteps above my head as he disappears behind his curtain.

I add wood to the fire and sip my Grand Marnier. Susannah and I used to drink the same liqueur when I worked at MacKenzie's bar in Oregon. I sit on the hard bench, alone in the *salle à manger*, missing Susannah, such an important friend, who came from a different world than I.

"My family was the only white family in Oakland," Susannah told me. A single mom with two children, she attended the community college, and volunteered at the White Bird crisis clinic in Eugene with me. "You wore that suede coat with fur," I told her later, "all hot in those tall boots, your hair the color of fire. You looked so damn sexy. I was a one-hundred-ninety-pound slug."

One night, with cigarette smoke and the scent of coffee wafting through the clinic, Susannah and I answered the crisis line phones together, both of us new volunteers. "You want to see some photos?" she asked, squeezing into my armchair. Though we'd trained side by side for two months, we'd never spoken.

"Sure."

I moved over in the chair, and she squished in next to me, and opened a package of snap shots (photos). "This is me." She pointed to a girl in red halter top and cut-offs, sitting on a Harley Davidson motorcycle. "And this is—was—my old man." A dude in black leathers kicked back on his bike. "We were on a ride last summer." Another photo showed twenty bikes, men and women, dudes and their ole' ladies, on Harleys. "Hey, what do you think about that guy who acts like a hard ass biker?" she asked, referring to our supervisor, who acted tough, but had, in fact two masters degrees. Her wicked sarcasm infected me, and we soon howled in laughter, though I secretly worshipped the guy, like half the volunteers did.

"I moved to Oregon," she said, "when a ton of friends OD'd on heroin." She sipped her coffee. "My parents were Oakies."

"Oakies?"

"You know. Left Oklahoma for California during the Dust Bowl."

Oh, yeah. Woody Guthrie. John Steinbeck.

"Neighborhood kids teased me for being fat when I was little," she said.

"Really. You?" I looked down at my own stomach rolls.

The light from the lamp softened her features, though her blue eyes focused like lasers. "But then I got skinny," she said. "And with my new body came men and jealous women, and fights in bars where I kicked some chick in the face, and smashed my old man over the head with a frying pan."

My eyebrows shot up. In my family, if someone were mad, they didn't talk for three days. We punished with the silent treatment. "I can't imagine you fat!" I said.

Her laugh was deep, infectious. "I ain't about to take shit from no one." Even if it meant barroom brawls, fights with the ex, laughing at the brainiac biker.

A year later, Susannah squeezed my hand, pumping it, when I pierced my nose. Another time, she brought me to the woods to cool off when I was flipping out. One summer, we hitchhiked to LA, and for better or worse, she introduced me to Garner. While Randy thinks about goats here on our French home, I think of Susannah and Garner. I guess I'm not such a pure goatherd, not like Randy, who definitely fits Eliot's description of 'purist' in *Adam Bede*.

After his nap, Randy beats eggs for a cheese soufflé, while I chop onions. The stove fire sputters as we try to maintain the temperature, the hardest part of creating a soufflé in a wood-burning stove. We peek, opening the iron door carefully to keep the soufflé from falling. The top grows puffy and slightly brown, and we remove it, ever so slowly. Success! It's scrumptious.

"I'm going to try to find an English station on the wireless," Randy says, after dishes.

"Randy!" No one has fiddled with the radio dial as long as we've lived here. It's always set to the same station for the broadcast news, talk radio, and of course, *Louisianne*. Randy drags a stool to the wall, reaches to the high shelf for the thirty-year-old box radio, sets it on the table, and brushes off the dust that's been collecting for god only knows how long. He turns the dial. Static.

I admire Randy. I, the American, always so eager to please the Fontaines, never even thought of touching their radio. Nor does it occur to me that we might be able to get an English station, which would be an utter joy. I'd love to hear English on the radio.

Randy turns the dial ever so slightly. We both hover over the radio, our ears down, close to the static, straining to hear, while Randy turns the dial just a smidgen at a time. He rotates the dial a little, again, and again, the tiniest little movement, and still static burns our ears. Finally, I give up. More power to him. "Good luck, Randy," I say. "I'm headed to bed." I slide under my blanket, listening to the crackling sounds from the radio, and soon the crackles begin to sound like words, and then clear speech comes through. English! Randy found an English broadcast!

"Randy!" I call down to him. "You did it. I can't believe it!" I'm shocked. "English on the radio!"

I try to hear every word. They're talking about the new electronic games with aliens, a quantum leap beyond "Pong." That Randy, I think. He found a treasure, hidden in plain sight. We've heard English pop songs on the French radio, over the past several months. Once, Randy and I counted—out of twelve songs on the French radio, two were French, ten, English, and most, American. But tonight, it's English people *speaking*!

With his imagination, his carefulness, and his persistence, he created a slight miracle. *Not bad,* I think, as I fall asleep learning more about video games than I ever cared to know.

In the morning, Randy rises at the proper time and herds the goats promptly at 8:00 a.m., just as he would if Camilla and Jacques were around. Where's the fun in that? I drag myself over to the pot of hot chicory and rub my eyes. God, Randy. Do you always have to be so good? Can't we at least sleep in?

Soon, I dress and bundle up for the cold, feed the chickens and the rabbits, give fresh water to the cow, and clean the house. Now, time to mend the Fontaine's pile of shirts and pants. Loneliness sweeps through me and I feel like an emptied-out bowl. Turning on my music helps lift my spirits a bit.

When I finish, it's time for my outside chores. A light snow falls, clinging to my hat, my gloves, and partway up my boots. I chop logs for firewood, and hike the hill for buckets of water, remembering the Buddhist saying. "What does a person do before Enlightenment? Chop wood and carry water. What does a person do after enlightenment? Chop wood and carry water."

With frozen fingers, I stretch one leg of my jeans along the laundry board outside of *la toilette* where the uneaten rabbits chatter behind the curtain. The wind swipes strands of my hair that slip out from under my hat, turning them to icicles while I scrub, scrub, scrub with the rough brush on a filthy knee of my jeans. With a bar of what my mother used to call "yellow soap," I rub until my raw knuckles morph from red to white, so cold they burn. Is it ten or fifteen below? And, with the wind chill factor? My fingers feel like they might just break in two, cold as they are. My jaw tightens when the winds jab my cheeks, and the bristles of the brush scratch my hands. The brown in the knees of my pants turns lighter, then blue-brown, then blue. I push those jeans to the side, and pull another pair from the bucket where it's soaking. My fingers stiffen like they have arthritis as I straighten the frozen pants, already hardened with ice in the short time I've been outdoors. I grasp the brush, barely able to bend my fingers, and scrub once again.

"Bonjour, *Ay liz a bet a.* Is Camilla here?"

I'm startled. "Oh, Marian." I set aside my work, glad, no, *relieved*, to have company. *"Bonjour."* Here we are, finally having a conversation. "Sorry, Marian. Camilla and Jacques left for a few days. They'll be back the day after tomorrow."

Marian nods. What more can I say? How can I keep our conversation going? I shift my feet. There must be some way to engage her. Marian remains still, a frozen lock of hair dancing over her forehead. She appears skinnier than ever, under the stretched grey sweater that hangs halfway to her knees.

"À toute à l'heure ," she says in her soft voice, a murmur, really, before she glides around the corner of the house. Damn. I wish I'd thought of something else to say. What's going on in this mysterious woman's mind?

I press the brush with all my weight, scrubbing my jeans as hard as I can. They say true growth is doing what you ought to do because you want to do it. Well, I sure don't want to be doing this, but I do want clean clothes, so here I am.

An old roommate once said, "The thing about monks is that they don't *do* anything. Sure, anyone can be spiritual who sits in cave, not dealing with people. Relating to people is the trick that tests our true spirituality. And maybe so, too, is scrubbing brittle jeans on a board in the icy mountain air.

That night, Randy and I chop tomatoes for the pizza we're making from scratch. "I think I'll stay here until March," I say. "I told Camilla I'd stay until spring and March seems long enough. I need to prove to myself that I can make it through this bloody winter."

I'm using Randy's words now. "Bloody!" What I don't say is that my mission was to learn to believe in myself, and every day that I survive these monstrous storms, I'm making progress. Little things I do, like my daily inspection of each goat for bruises, bumps, or irregularities spell that I'm becoming a better person. I feel closer to my higher self and I've learned the magic of hard work.

Chop, chop, chop. I layer slices of tomatoes on the pizza dough that Randy made this morning. "I've been wondering what I'm going to do when I leave," I say. Randy stirs the wood to maintain a steady temperature and I slip in the pizza. "You know what I've been thinking about? I think I'd like to go to Morocco when I leave."

With barely moving lips, Randy says, "Mmm. I'll probably leave before then."

Ohhh. We've never talked about our leaving the farm at the same time, never talked about traveling together, but somehow I've been fantasizing that we might. Maybe even go to Morocco together. Sure, he's young and inexperienced, but I don't want to go alone.

It quits snowing the following day, but even so, the goats and I must hike over a mile to find leaves and nuts. I slip and slide on the sometimes muddy, sometimes frozen trail, passing leafless trees where the goats grazed in the past. The goats follow one another with the clump of sheep lagging behind. When we reach open plains of rock and thyme, the goats begin to scatter until they find there's food to be found. I call *"Allez, allez"* and they come, and follow me over the hill where we'd see the Mediterranean on a clear day, but today, only miles of fog.

I scratch Coconut's head and feel her pregnant belly, growing larger every day. My newest indulgence, Jane Austen's *Pride and Prejudice,* is especially hard to put down. I've heard women say they were "soooo in love" with Mr. Darcy. But, it's Elizabeth Bennet who intrigues me. I'd like to be her: intelligent, bright, witty. She has that balance of confidence and belief in herself, without being haughty and conceited. The book reminds me that I rarely attempt activities which truly challenge me—like writing a book, for example—because if or when I fail, my pride will be crushed. I write three times a day in my journal. Nobody sees that. Show my writing? I won't do that. Could it be that my *not* writing a book is rooted in vanity?

After their three-day excursion, Camilla and Jacques return to a clean house and well-cared-for animals. Camilla immediately rakes through the trash to figure out what happened in their absence. I can't imagine what she expects to find. Old routines are restored as though the Fontaines never left, which was actually okay, because life was getting boring and monotonous without them. What did I expect being alone for three days with Randy? I'm not sure.

Chapter Twelve
Visiting

Camilla surprises me by asking if Randy and I would like to go visiting. Again? For no reason? Yes, certainly. Camilla has never invited us to socialize other than Christmas Eve. But she has softened—I work faster, and she criticizes less, and we are becoming friends. We set out in the truck, our odd trio: Camilla, with her friend (me) and her friend's shy friend (Randy). Is he my boyfriend or my brother? Who knows? Randy remains silent. Smug? Shy?

We first visit Marian's brother in a *très petit* village. I learn that hundreds of years ago, the houses were clumped together—four or six—for protection from invaders. That's why we'll come upon a village of a small batch of houses dotting miles and miles of open countryside.

Marian's brother's house is dark. There is no electricity. The Fontaines, with their two dangling light bulbs, are one of the few in this area who have electricity. The fire at Marian's brothers offers a bit of light, and the yellow flames warm us all. "Ah, Marian," I say. We kiss each other's cheeks, and I park myself next to her on the hearth, while the others—six strangers to me—chat too rapidly for me to understand. Marian listens without speaking. I watch the lively conversation, always theatrical with the hands and arms, as communicative as words. I like sitting near Marian, even if we don't say more than a few words. Her thin, white hand sets her wine glass on the floor, and she folds her fingers, her nails bitten to shreds.

After nearly an hour, Camilla rises, brushes her pants. "Time to go," she says like a Girl Scout leader. When I kiss Marian's cheeks to say *à toute à l'heure*, her green eyes appear moist. *"Bonne nuit, Ay liz a bet a."* Marian rarely calls me by my name. Her voice sounds like an echo in a cave, remote.

As we drive past rows and rows of vineyards, I crouch into my seat. *"Bonne nuit, Ay liz a bet a,"* she'd said, sounding melodic. I gaze into the night; the only light on the road emitted from our headlights. Marian had grasped her hands so tightly. She wasn't gorgeous like Marie, but rather, lovely—delicate like the fine china we used for *fêtes*. I scanned the outline of the mountains, unable to shake her drawn face from my mind.

"Alors," Camilla interrupts my reverie. "We're here." We knock and enter the home of a German couple who have a luxury I haven't seen in more than half a year. Oh, yes, I've forgotten the comfort: a *couch!* Big, soft, and comfy. Well, it isn't that big, and perhaps not so soft, but it's so much more comfortable than the stone hearth and wooden benches that I've been sitting on since September. I drop into the cushion, and close my eyes for just a moment, relaxing in its folds. My! Couches! What a great invention.

My German host pours me a glass of wine, while Camilla and the others chatter, their hands dancing. I understand little. The German knows English, but only speaks French.

The next morning I'm astonished to see sun, a magnificent orb, glowing red like the coals in our fire. Last night's visits recharged me. I'm invigorated. I gather thyme for dinner while I herd, sing to myself, and skip with Elusive along a ridge. A flock of birds wisps overhead and once again, I'm awed by the beauty of the shimmering line on the horizon, the Mediterranean Sea, many miles away. "*Allez,*" I call as Elusive runs ahead, and Coconut lags behind. Back at the barn, everyone settles in easily. I feel at peace under the blue sky dome with its thin, drifting clouds.

I hear the phone ring right before I enter the house. A shriek suddenly explodes, a scream that churns my blood. I fly into the kitchen where the howl, "*NONNNNNN*" continues. Camilla buries her face in her hands. I rush in and throw my arms around her in a tight hug. Her eerie wail fades to a whimper. Tears streak her face. Her glasses slide down her nose. She hugs me back. Randy, Louis, and Marie clamor down the ladder to hear what's going on. The wood in the fire snaps. Camilla's lips tremble and she says, "*C'est Marian.* It's Marian. Marian killed herself."

The phone in the *salle à manger* lies on the floor. My knees feel like they're melting, and can barely hold me up. Marian? My God. Marian? I'm stunned. Why? Why would our strong, gentle Marian kill herself? Marian, the friend I almost had. I suck in my lips, holding my feelings, damming the currents of tears ready to fall, ready to flood. No, not

Marian. The woman who peels a full apple with one twist of the wrist, releasing the peel with one quick stroke. How could she?

I think, *I should have known.* Contradictory thoughts jumble in my mind. On the one hand, she always seemed so elegant, so sure of herself. On the other, last night she seemed so sad. I try to comprehend. *Marian killed herself.* It doesn't seem possible.

Camilla takes her coat from the hook. "I'm going to Jean's," she says, her voice raspy. I wipe my eyes, curl my hair behind my ears.

My mind flashes to scenes of Marian: standing alone at the dance, peeling her apples, laughing at our Christmas *fête*, and then, quiet at their miserably cold house on New Year's Day. Last night her face seemed etched in pain. How long had she been thinking about killing herself? Oh, why, dear Marian?

Now, alone in the kitchen I ask myself, what can I do? In this remote world, there is one answer to every question: work. Randy leaves with the goats. In my five months on the farm, I've perfected the routine. I gather wood and stack it against the wall-to-wall fireplace, haul buckets of water from the source, feed an injured goat who remains in the barn, and finally, begin my trek toward Marian's and Jean's village. Halting midway, I remember the dishes and retrace my steps. When I hang up my drying towel, and put away the clean dishes, Marie and Louis burst in the kitchen. "The doctor drove us home," Louis says, panting. "The village is filled with police and an ambulance." A flame shatters a branch in the fireplace.

I put on an extra sweater, then two layers of coats, and trod up the road where the green, rocky hills roll ahead of the blue mountains, semi-transparent, like a watercolor painting, just a shade darker than the pale sky. Glaciers shine on the snow-covered mountains. I'm struck by the incongruity of the beauty on this narrow, empty road and the tragedy of Marian's death. How can I be walking in such magnificence when I feel like a knife is stabbing my heart?

Death by a shotgun. I picture Marian last night, her grey sweater hanging from her shoulders, her voice sad when she spoke. "*Bonne nuit, Ay liz a bet a.*"

When I arrive in her village, I first see two policemen, official in their blue, round hats, standing rigid, in the middle of the dusty road. Arms crossed, clubs in their pockets, the edges of their hats sharp, their demeanor cold.

Once I'd read about officious mannerisms—that a person can transform from humane to inhumane, from personal to wicked authority, with the garb of "official decorum." I swallow and inch forward. "*Arrêtez!*" a policeman shouts to me. "Go back!"

I wait on a boulder on the other side of the road, facing Jean and Marian's house, hoping there will be some way to help. New troops arrive, more men in blue, austere beyond my comprehension. The blood in my veins feels frozen. I am stiff, unmoving, unbelieving. I wait. And wait.

A wooden wheelbarrow, rickety, comes into view, pushed adeptly, with purpose. It seems ironic that the first movement in this shocking drama is a brown, wobbly wheelbarrow, piled high with a mound of hay. Camilla pushes it past me, waving as a trail of slender stalks falls to the road. An officer approaches her. She stops, leaves her wheelbarrow, and departs with him, presumably for more questioning. Will Marian's animals eat today?

Jean appears, his face white and dry, his jowls flushed, like a corpse with rouge applied to his cheeks. His actions are exacting, precise. He lifts the handles of the wheelbarrow, and passes a few feet from me. He nods; half smiles, and mouths, "*Bonjour.*" His voice, his eyes, the curvature of his mouth, seem sour, bitter. More than sadness, more than fear, anxiety, or cold, hard pain, Jean appears to be unimaginably bitter. That is the irony. He, who suffers most, whose wife is dead, is kicked at, hawked at, and accused. Or so it seems, as I watch. I'm a bystander, interpreting faces, movements, dark, dark eyes.

Jean proceeds down the hill with the wheelbarrow. The police pursue him, as though he might run or escape, though clearly there is no exit in the surrounding miles of barren hills, speckled only with rocks and thyme and sage. He pushes open his wooden gate, every muscle in his hands, his arms, and his neck supporting his head, strained, hardened like iron, weighted under the skin. His movements seem crystallized, punctuated in pain.

What is true here, I do not know. I feel my sadness rise like a storm, a small tornado, swirling within me. I amble home, alone on the deserted road, once again struck by the contrast of the azure sky, lovely, and my splintered emotions. A car rolls by, driven by the wife of Marian's brother. Her pale face, marked with scrawny plucked eyebrows, holds no glamour. I never liked that woman. Anjilique, I believe, is her name. But today, as her eyes pin to the road, her mouth shrivels to a taut "O," vacant, determined—today, her shock and despair overwhelm me.

I reflect, again, on the previous evening, when Camilla and I remarked on Marian's melancholy; Marian's eyes, when she kissed my cheeks and said "*Bonne nuit, Ay liz a bet a;*" her tenderness when we sat beside each other before the sputtering fire; our exchange, in which I felt a shyness. Yes, perhaps she had betrayed her intentions.

How do we survive the chilling death of our family's closest friend? Steadfast routine. One foot in front of the other. Marian's death devastated us all, but it hit Camilla hardest, like a hollow pit dug deep into her soul. I'd envied Marian's grace, the loveliness that shone through her ragged sweater and torn jeans when she floated through our wine-scented kitchen on her frequent visits to Camilla. I longed for her friendship. I, the American, herding goats on a whim, and she, a thirty-two year old French woman, barely surviving. Day after day, she'd stand stiff, her hands clasped behind her back, while the fire in the *salle à manger* flamed behind her, shooting sparks like pieces of her soul. Would we converse even if we spoke the same language? Would we share feelings of being wounded, of aching, of carrying on despite our tumultuous emotions? Is that what drew Marian to me? A bruised and broken heart? It's subtle, that attraction of wounded to wounded, and yet, we often find and heal each other, just by being present.

Tonight Randy chops leeks for the soup as I wash dirt off the carrots. The never-ending wind flings open the back door, and Jacques enters, his blue eyes crystal clear. Something more, something horrible, has happened.

Randy and I struggle to understand Jacques' French. "Jean has been officially charged with her murder." The children run into the kitchen. "*Oui, oui.* Everyone is saying Jean killed Marian." I turn, trying to escape the news as I set the table. No. Not Jean. He couldn't have.

As we prepare the table, Camilla speaks more quietly than I've ever heard her. "*Non.* Last year Marian tried to hang herself," she said.

Marie phones her friends. I listen, her words falling too fast for me to catch, to understand exactly, but her meaning is clear. Her voice hushes with a touch of glee, perhaps, as though part of her relishes the gossip. "Yes, Marian is dead," Marie says. "It's true. Marian put a shotgun in her mouth. She put a shotgun in her mouth and pulled the trigger. *Oui*, just this morning. *Oui,* her husband Jean found her. *Oui, je ne peux pas imaginer.* I can't imagine. And some say, no, it was not like that. Jean killed her."

The bench squeaks against the cement as I scoot it forward, gazing aimlessly into the fire. When Marie speaks of Marian, I think how easy it is to trivialize such tragedy when you're just fourteen years old. An hour later, when Marie and I crawl into bed, I realize how grief-stricken she truly is. How hard she takes Marian's death. "*J'ai peur,*" she says. "I am afraid."

The rain thrashes the roof, inches above our heads. We lie awake, our minds whirling in wonder. What happened to Marian? Why did she do it? Poor Marie. Encapsulated, Marie's been protected on this serene goat farm. Now, her world has cracked. Her shell of safety burst, and she's now discovered torment and despair.

In the morning, Camilla stirs the stew for dinner, her wooden spoon rings against the pot like a deep sounding bell. Dressed in her blue shoulder-to-waist apron, Camilla says to me, "Marian had courage to kill herself." Courage? A sharp needle shoots through my chest. Marian was Camilla's closest friend in the world. Courage?

We hear a knock at the kitchen door. Two men and a woman, dressed in navy wool coats and boots, rugged yet elegant in their handsome wool scarves, ask to use the phone. Camilla has the only phone on this road of tiny villages. Though her friends once criticized her for bringing in "*les choses modernes*," everyone feels comfortable stopping by to use these modern things. The guests scrape their boots at the entrance, tossing off clotted dirt. Two of the visitors are originally from England, and the other, from Germany. Now in their early thirties, they migrated to southern France around ten years ago as part of the back to nature movement, during the early seventies.

Had Marian dreamed of utopia when she moved here, like these foreign visitors? A dream that ended with a shotgun shell? A dream that did not include the vicious winds and the snow of the mountain winters, that overlooked treks for buckets of water, and hikes to find wood for the fire? A dream that ignored the loneliness, the despair, and the wicked cold? Camilla sniffs, rubs her red nose. "I feel guilty," she tells me. Guilt is such a human reaction. It allows us to put cause and effect, action and reaction, neatly into a box, so we can say, "If only I had done x, y, z, then…" No. Guilt doesn't apply here.

"Have you had a chance to cry?" I ask Camilla. She answers, yes, she cried a lot.

"Many families here are disillusioned with life," she says. "They feel listless, disappointed that their 'vitality' depends on money." Vitality does not mean Disneyland or trips to Florida. Vitality means water and food and warmth.

Back on the hillside, the day after our conversation, the clouds remind me of white sheets flapping in the breeze. The goats and their tinkling bells provide sanctuary, as I muse on Jean. His wife, dead by a shotgun and he, accused. Jean, who used to stop by nearly every day, now stays away. Does Jean force himself to get out of bed in his icy stone home, to gather wood, to build a fire, or does he shiver, watch his frozen breath, watch his tears form icicles? He stays alone, declines invitations for dinner. I imagine him in the same room, the same bed, where he slept with Marian, night after night, his eyes glued to the ceiling, following each crack in the plaster, each spider's web. Does his mind reel like a broken record, dwelling on their last hours together, the last bitter words of her defeated life, the last time she looked into his face?

My life has been too simple, too dreadfully easy. No one close to me has died. Jean's emotions are beyond my grasp. I pray God will soothe him.

Five days after Marian's death, another blizzard sweeps in. Back at the house, after a frigid day, I fill a bucket with boiling water and carry it into the *fromagerie,* the cheese-drying room, and sit in a straight-back wooden chair. With no baths, this is my luxury: soaking my feet. The misery of herding my goats in the cold, wet snow barely touches me now as I grieve for Marian and worry about Jean.

A week passes. Jacques rides his horse to fetch Jean for dinner. This time Jean accepts the invitation. Spoons knock against our soup bowls, wine glasses tap the table. We drink our soup, self-conscious, and talk about everything but the one thing we're all thinking about. I overcompensate, acting at ease by joking. Of course, that doesn't work.

Jean's cheek bones protrude, black rings circle his eyes. By the end of the meal, perhaps because of his wine, he lightens up, if only a bit. Mr. Bawdy from across the street barges in, screaming and shouting, turning the *salle à manger* into a three-ring circus with forced *joie de vivre.*

Back on the hills with the goats that afternoon, I pray, and feel some solace. In the icy winds, Ma Rosa looks like a bull, her eyes intent and horns pointed. When she throws back her head, I step away. She terrifies me more and more.

The weather reverses itself the next day, warming us once again. I carry a tray of the oldest cheese, small mounds covered with the dark, blue-green scaly mold, outdoors. I cut the mold off the mounds with a fine knife, careful not to cut the cheese buried underneath. The oldest, most valuable cheese is aged and sharp, about three-quarters of an inch thick and two inches in diameter. Randy, on his day off, comes outside, surprising me. "I think Morocco would be a nice place to visit." He speaks slowly, tentatively, in his Australian drawl.

"You want to travel together?" I ask, trying to sound cool but feeling ecstatic. Randy, traveling with me to Morocco? *Yes!* I feel both the depths of sadness about Jean and Marian, and at the same time, euphoric about traveling to Morocco with Randy.

"When shall we go? March?"

"I was hoping to leave before that," Randy says.

I start on another mound of cheese. "I said I'd stay 'til spring." The green mold I slice off is ugly. "I can't leave before March."

That night, life has a sense of normalcy as we assemble around the table after supper, the fire cracking, and Louis and Marie across from one another, books open, pencils to paper, working on school assignments. Camilla sews her curtains; Randy studies his stamp collection, luring me to his passion. We examine all the stamps on the cards and letters I've been sent from the USA. We trade. We admire. We laugh. Stamp collecting seems like an anachronism—an austere, useless hobby, but I participate with fervor, although in the end, my stamps will remain in the envelope, untouched. We huddle close to the candles, the dim, yellow light flickering on our projects.

"No school," Camilla tells Louis in the morning. "There's been another blizzard." To me, Camilla says, "Feed the animals in the barn, and then bring *le bébé* back in the house."

Randy and I tramp to the barn through snow up to our thighs. "Let's put hay in all the corners," says Randy, "so everyone has enough to eat." We're besieged by clanging bells, little goats and big ones, the sheep, and the cow, all hungry. We scatter the hay, so even the *très petits* get their share.

I loop the rope around the neck of the big-eyed calf, still so cute with his stilt-like legs, and lead him to the house where he trots over the doorstep, and claps his hoofs on our stone floor, prancing around the *salle à manger*. "*Ay liz a bet a,*" Camilla says, "Time to darn." Darn socks? Once again, I feel like I'm time traveling back in time, back to the Ponderosa. She pulls what looks like a wooden egg from the sewing kit, and tucks it into a blue sock with a hole in its toe. "*Voici.*" She threads a thick needle with yarn that matches the color and weight of the sock, and weaves a row of stitches first above the hole, then through it, and finally below. After tying off the yarn, she begins again in the perpendicular direction, weaving above, through, and below. It reminds me of weaving those six-inch square potholders at summer camp. I feel like such a grown woman, darning socks in front of the fire, while Camilla makes goat cheese on this cold and snowy day.

It's as good a time as any to broach the subject. "Randy and I will be leaving together in March." Jacques drops his eyes and winces. I'm going to miss the Fontaines—we've become so close. But, I also feel liberated—finally, sun, a new adventure, Morocco! Camilla nods, stirs her milk on the stove, and says nothing.

I am free to leave. I'm almost ready to move on.

Heavy rain and snow closes all the roads to and from our village. A German man, who had been riding his horse, knocks on the door dripping wet. Jacques welcomes him, and offers a glass of wine. Are all these visitors strangers, just passing by, or are they old friends? I'm never quite clear. But, everyone is welcome.

Mr. Bawdy and his wife burst in, shouting once again, as our little calf prances anxiously and repeatedly around the table. All of us squeeze together as close to the warm fire as we can: I darn, the German and Jacques drank their wine, and Bawdy bellows on and on. Our baby calf didn't eat yesterday, or in the morning, but when the German and Bawdy call him, he trots over, suddenly a gregarious fellow. He nuzzles everyone, accepts head rubs, and finally, drinks out of the milk bottle. He looks up at the visitors, his biggest audience yet, and guzzles all his milk. *Le bébé* is a social butterfly.

The weather humbles me. The next day, out in another storm, I try to wiggle my toes and fingers while I herd. They are numb. Icy winds slash snow across my nose, my cheeks. I'd cry if I had the strength.

Sorrow can find you anywhere, I think, even up on the mountains of Languedoc surrounded by goats. Usually, I hide from my grief with books, but I can't hold in these feelings in this brutal weather. Like pot, TV, and alcohol, books are like drugs, shielding me from true feelings. Unlike those other drugs, books fortify me—make me stronger, reinvigorated, maybe, even wiser. Great books help me escape. They redirect my thoughts, and I'd like to have them redirected this morning. This afternoon I'm attending my very first funeral.

Once again, the snow reaches over our boots, up to our knees, as we all trudge from the house to the car. Louis crams into the far back, bending his head and neck forward against the ceiling. I squeeze in the middle seat, lucky to have the warmest place, in between Marie and Randy, who each lean against the freezing doors. In the front, Camilla sits stiffly, ignoring the children's squabbles, as Jacques maneuvers the icy roads.

"Papa! Papa!" Louis cries out. Faithful Natasha is chasing the car, her mouth part open, her tail wagging. *"Arrête! Papa!"* Jacques checks out the rear view mirror, slows the car, and Natasha jumps in the back with Louis, who pats and chatters with the dog for the remainder of the ride.

I've never been to a funeral. Never. Now I worry about my tendency to laugh at the worst possible moments, when I'm scared or nervous. Without snow tires, the car slides on the ice. I wring my hands as we cross over the hills that rise and fall in dunes of snow, musing on the meaning of Marian's death. It's more than the loss of a friend. It's losing hope in a lifestyle, in a new way of life that was supposed to be better than the city life of greed and materialism.

The car reaches a crest, surrounded by snow drifts that look like pillows on all sides. Below us, in the valley, we see the tiny, grey stone church, with a parking lot on one side and a cemetery on the other. The church looks about two hundred years old. Generations of men piled the stones of its walls on top of one another, by hand.

We steady ourselves, skating across the icy parking lot, listening to the whispers of other people heading in. We steal into the silent, dark church, each of our steps reverberating on the floor of stone, the same stones as the walls. Jean meets us at the door and leads us through the dark to our seats. We sit in the first row. The first row? We're Marian's closest family. A single ray of sun spotlights the seats when the door opens in the rear. Michel and his friend enter and join us in our pew. I tighten my scratchy scarf around my neck, clasp my frozen hands together, and watch my breath rise in white wisps.

The priest, robed in black, stands directly in front of us, begins to speak in foreign words with a voice that honks, nasally, grotesque. I peer over my shoulder, noting the pews are scarcely filled. Almost choking on the dense incense, I chew my lips. The priest finishes. A cough sounds from the back of the church.

We follow the priest down the center of the dark aisle, scuffing the stone floor, inching through the viscous air, laden with smoke and desolation, as tangible as the cold of our fingers. Icy drips fall from our noses. Jean and Jacques and Louis and Michel lift the casket and carry it out of the church. Following alone and in pairs, we leave the dark church and blink at the bright, grey daylight, a sharp contrast to our eyes. We mill through the snow behind the church until we reach the spot where they place the casket, in front of a simple white cross. We no longer muffle our tears. Sobs, loud and fierce, sound even more poignant against hardened, icy snow. The casket can't be buried. The ground is frozen. Instead, we stare at the brown wooden box while the priest utters a few more words.

The crowd is small: men and women in black coats and boots, women with scarves covering their heads and ears, men with woolen caps. They all turn and hobble back to their cars. I trail the mourners to the parking lot, then veer away from our car, to be alone, to separate myself from the family, to immerse myself in the white mountains surrounding me on all sides. Sadness wells within me. It feels eerily familiar—as though I knew this sorrow all my life. At least since my teenage years.

I grew up with a modicum of privilege: Caucasian, prep school, college, the Cape. But I've felt alone and ugly and fat and ashamed and rejected. I buried all those feelings, buried them under cookies and ice cream, alcohol and drugs. And now, suddenly, in this icy parking lot with frozen toes and a runny nose, I honor those raw emotions, so deeply entrenched in my being—feelings that I hid from myself while I walled myself off, so I never had to feel this pain. I feel it now. Years of buried emotions burst through the dam, here in this tiny parking lot in the mountains of Languedoc, next to this old, stone church.

My eyebrows tighten in anger. Why are we shocked by Marian's death? Suddenly I want to go funerals, lots of funerals, where one is allowed to feel despair openly. Permission is granted. I picture Marian, thin and pallid, maybe truly starving, because she had so little money. I'm bitter about people's blindness and remember the quote, whose origin I do not know: "You are consumed in your faith in justice." Yes, I believe in the ultimate good, but there is no justice. Inside my head, I am screaming, it's all unfair; it's all unfair! As I wail, my burden lightens.

I breathe the glacial air in the church parking lot, and rejoin my French family. Together we crowd into the car and swerve through the hills back home. Jean eats dinner with us. Though his face is sallow, his eyes dull, he seems to have the will to live. Color returns to his face. Dinner conversation is trite, trivial, until Louis asks innocently enough, "Who made the cross for the grave?"

Now I can no longer hold my unwanted giggles. Laughing at the wrong time, wrong place has been the bane of my existence. I bite my cheek as hard as I can to muffle my giggles. I have behaved respectfully up to now. But I can't imagine someone in America asking, "Who made the headstone; who made the cross?" But, then again, I've no experience with funerals, headstones, or crosses.

"I did," replies Jean. "I made the cross."

How does one respond to a compliment on the cross you made for your dead wife's grave?

Marian's suicide crushes the Fontaine household. Each of us finds our own way of dealing with it: tears, spiritual reflection, routine, and work. We each move in a quiet, slow motion of gloom. Outside, rain gushes and monsoon-like winds hack the thin trees.

My feelings mirror the vile weather. Some people believe we peel off layer upon layer of our exterior selves, to reach our true core, our soul, our God-self. My grieving sheds layers, and underneath is my innermost being, where a new spirit of love has grown. I feel compassion, especially for Camilla, who carries on and yet still seems lost, ravaged by the loss of her closest friend.

A few days after the funeral, I navigate my herd through pathways swollen with puddles, stopping to find the rare trees with leaves. My herd and I shiver together. We shouldn't be out here. The storm is far too nasty. When we're two-thirds of the way home, the goats bolt back to the barn, then cling together as closely as the sheep, trying to warm and dry each other. Returning to the *salle à manger* without an inch of dry skin, I hang up my drenched clothes in front of the fire. "*Ay liz a bet a*," asks Camilla, "Would you like to go to Beziers with me this afternoon?" Does Camilla feel guilty about having me herd in the torrential rains? Is that why she asked me to go with her? Or does she want company, a friend, to travel with through the squall? Our roles have changed over the past few weeks. Now, I'm more her friend than her employee.

"*Mais, oui.*" I'd love a change in scene. But the winds and the rains never let up for the whole trip to Beziers and back. There's no heater in the car. I hold my arms across my chest to warm myself. When we arrive back home, we wade through icy puddles to the freezing house where the scent of peppery potato soup greets us, the only warmth in this dismal day. We eat supper in silence. We sit in silence afterward. Even the bones of the house are in mourning.

The day after we travel to Beziers, the temperature rises a bit, and I feel a change, as though I've accepted Marian's death. Whether she killed herself, or whether Jean killed her, barely matters to me. Either is equally tragic. I don't want to wonder if Jean murdered her. It is too painful, too disconcerting, too awful to imagine. Yet, possible. I allow that. He may have shot her. And as soon as that thought comes to mind, I block it out again. Remembering she tried to hang herself last year, I dismiss the idea of Jean shooting her.

In the evening, I try to read *The Reivers* by William Faulkner. Though laced with touches of humor, it presents societies' conflicts in class, race, and modernization. When I first picked up the book, I got bored, and put it down. Tonight, though, I'm captivated by Faulkner's way of looking at the gray lines separating virtue and non-virtue. I laugh aloud at parts, glued until I finish the book.

The scent of Randy's rice pudding draws me to the kitchen where we chat, listening to Van Morrison sing, *It's a marvelous night for a moon dance* on the tape player. Camilla appears, in from the blustery outdoors, shaking the rain from her coat. I can't construe the odd expression on her face.

"*Ay liz a bet a*, Randy," Camilla says with tense lips, dull eyes, her hair dripping from the rain, "I'm going away for a while." Randy and I glance at each other.

"For how long?" I ask.

"A while. A few weeks."

I shift my weight from one foot to another, scratch my head. Randy stands straighter, his hands still, frozen. I guess she and Jacques and the children have already discussed her departure, but I am shocked.

Camilla gone? Camilla, our axis? Her sadness is palpable. She is not recovering from Marian's death. She needs to get away. We can see that. I say, "We'll miss you." I hear the rain pummel the door, the metal lid rattle on the pot on the stove. "I hope you have a good trip."

Herd on the mountainside

Beautiful sausages like bells

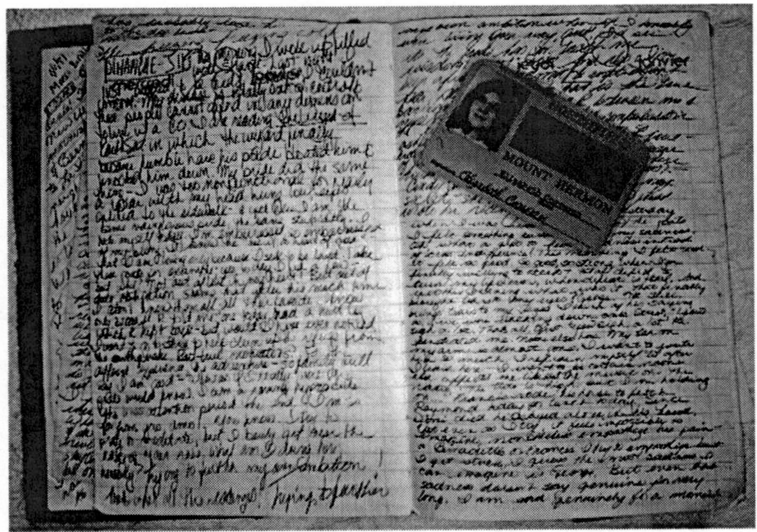

Journal from the winter of 1980-81 with prep school ID card

Elizabeth with her goats

PART III. Winter's Heart

In every winter's heart, there is a quivering spring; and behind the veil of each night, there is a smiling dawn.

-Kahlil Gibran

Part III. Winter's Heart

Chapter Thirteen

New Morning

Camilla leaves by noon. I set the table for dinner, Randy serves the curry soup, and Jacques munches on his bread. Jacques pours another glass of wine, listening to *Louisianne*. While the absence of Camilla sits between us, in an odd way, dinner seems almost routine. We will carry on.

In the early morning shadows, my alarm jars me from another night of restless sleep. I roll over, bang the clock, and rub my eyes. Where's Camilla? How is she? How will we do without her, the hub of our little world? Yes, she criticizes and argues, but she befriended me on the day of the dance, on Christmas Eve, and on the evening we went visiting before Marian died. Though the bath was a disaster, she was motivated by kindness when she arranged it. Thoughts of her early criticisms ebb when I think of her generosity.

I dress, pulling my jeans over my long underwear. In the kitchen, I shove logs into the kitchen stove, and light scraps of paper, which I blow on in order to create small flames. The sweet smell of burning oak fills the room. I begin to brew the coffee chicory.

Moving to the *salle à manger*, I add a log and blow on last night's embers, hoping the fire will burn throughout the day. If the fire dies, the inside temperature will dip below freezing. Success is when we can't see our breath indoors. With only fourteen logs left, Jacques will need to hunt for wood today.

"Louis, Marie, come on down. Time to get ready for school," I call up to the lofts. Back in the kitchen, I pour the boxed milk into a pan over the wood stove, and stir in the chocolate mix. When Camilla said she was leaving, I knew what it would mean. I would be in charge. Yes, Randy will help with meals, and is the prime person for the goats, just as Jacques is the prime person for the horses. But, they're not the ones who'll keep the household going.

"*Merci*," the children whisper, wiping crust from their tired eyes as they drink their hot chocolate.

"I'm going to get some water," I say. In my coat, hat, and mittens, I slide up the icy path, slick like oil, to the source. By the time I'm back with two full buckets, Randy is skimming the cream from the cow's milk, which we'll sell up the road.

Louis and Marie hustle out the door for school. *"A tout l'heure."*

"A tout l'heure."

"Well, Randy," I ask, "How do you think we're going to do without Camilla?"

"Awlright," he drawls as he dresses in layers of coats to wear while he herds. Soon after, he departs for the hills, Jacques leaves to search for wood.

I hold my cup with both hands like I'm in a Folgers coffee commercial. "Okay, house, it's you, me, and the chores." Like being on automatic, I plan my day, order my list, and prioritize my tasks. Scouring the sauce pan, I imagine myself for a moment as being part of a family with children. I've rarely thought about having children, but, now I like the idea of being a mom with kids.

I feed hay to Charlie, the goat who hurt his leg, and to our quickly growing calf. They both coo and call, a bit mournfully. "You're pretty cute, Charlie," I say, patting the fella. He tucks his head between my legs, ever grateful for the food. "And you," I say to the calf, "You look like a giant baby boy in your cute, stumbling, awkward way." His saucer eyes stare up in appreciation.

Alone in the dung-filled, cold barn, with just the animals, I feel differently than I do with humans. Naked, no pretension, no judgments, just *being*, like all these little critters. Is this why Randy likes being with the goats so much? Because with them, he can be so thoroughly and completely authentic? Like Garner. So few people are as emotionally naked, as genuine, as Garner. What a sense of peace comes from just being. I'm so glad I discovered that feeling of authenticity without him, here in the isolated mountains of Languedoc.

Frost forms like little snowballs in the corners of the Fontaine's barn. I return to the kitchen, where I collect food scraps and swing the handle of the green bucket, making my way to the rabbits' cage. "Here you go," I say to the white-spotted bunny in *la toilette*. "When will we eat you?" My finger sticks through his cage, and touch his moist, twitching nose. "I bet you're wondering the same thing." He nibbles on the food scraps, watching me with his dark, shiny eyes. Next, it's on to the chicken coop where I scatter the rest of the food before returning to the house.

Now the indoor chores: I stir ashes, add wood, and blast the Stones,' *Exile on Main Street*, great music for slicing potatoes. After that, it's time to chuck the potatoes and leeks into the pot for soup, and settle into my favorite spot on the hearth to darn Marie's socks.

Why is it scary to be responsible? Because it means believing in myself? I weave thick, red yarn over the sock's hole, smelling the wine-scented soup. I'm such a contradiction. In fact, I was a prefect at Northfield-Mt. Hermon; a leader at White Board clinic; a member of the Board of Directors; presented before the Eugene Zoning Commission in support of mental health facilities; volunteered in countless positions. I did take charge. And yet still, where is my confidence? It's like something is blocking me.

"Ow!" My finger bleeds a drop from the prick. I once dreamed that Camilla was my professor, a lecturer in a huge university, writing on the blackboard. Which makes sense, really. Camilla taught me to love work, to order my time and possessions, to be fast and efficient. Managing the farm, caring for the children, and sharing responsibility with Randy, tests me like the final exam from my professor of life.

Sometimes I'd prefer to be a child again, not to be tested like this. And yet, what an opportunity! To run the farm. To prove myself. It's a gift. I stick the darning needle in Marie's red sock. I'll do fine, I reassure myself. I'll do just fine.

The hands spin around the clock, and Randy sticks his head in the door, done herding for the day. "Ready to milk?"

"Yep."

Inside the barn, Randy throws me a rope to tie Ma Rosa's head. I plunk down on the overturned bucket that serves as a stool and squeeze the teats, first one, then the other, and back again. The milk squirts with a swish into the bucket, filling it almost to the rim.

"Randy, check it out," I say. "The most I've ever gotten." Randy squeezes a few more times, and in the end, we've collected a full bucket of milk.

Jacques unloads his cart of wood, and carries it to the *salle à manger*. Randy makes butter, shaking the milk in the jar until his arms throb, while I cook supper—fried rice, onions, celery, and eggs. Randy, our culinary aficionado, adds ham. Though we're always horribly cold and wet, the dark pall shrouding the family's spirits lifts. The children laugh instead of fight, and Jacques smiles at their quips. My shoulders relax. "Dinner is delicious," Louis says, and the others nod.

Day one of Camilla's absence: success. Randy and I work in synch, like an old married couple. Marian's death remains with us, but with tortured Camilla away, we move beyond our mourning.

The next day I lead my herd to a new place which Jacques showed me, on the other side of the hills, where foliage still abounds. This spot is saved for the dead of winter. The faster goats dart ahead, the little ones trot near me, and the older ones stagger behind. As always, the nameless sheep move in a giant swath in the middle. Jacques waves *a tout a l'heure,* and I settle in, turning my face to the radiant sun, a miracle after the recent spate of storms. "*Je bois le soleil,*" Michel, the absent brother, once said to me. "I drink the sunshine."

My sheep remind me of characters at a cocktail party who stand off by themselves, content with each other, but with no interest in anyone else. They cluster together, rarely wander off, but have no desire to interact. They are in a world of their own. Until today.

A sheep lies prone a few dozen feet from me. That's odd. Sheep rarely lie down. She must be sick. I walk over to her, and rub her steel wool hair. There's a spot of blood, and examining more closely, I see two tiny hooves peek out. The ewe is so furry, we didn't know she was pregnant!

Oh, my God. There's no one else nearby, and we're far from the barn and the house. It's up to me! I get down on my knees to bend over the sheep. I take off my coat and push up my sleeves, and get to work. "Okay, Mama." I rub her belly, and the two tiny hoofs emerge a few more inches. "It's okay. Push! Push!" She cries out and heaves and pushes and pushes. I reach in as gently as possible, and feel gooey legs. "Come on! You can do it." The mama groans again. "Okay, take a break." The Mama looks worn. "One more time!" I pull the wet sticky legs until they emerge, and then I feel the body. Mama pushes one final time and almost miraculously a little baby lamb slips out onto the grass. I hear the bells from the herd, ringing like a choir, congratulating the Mama sheep who worked so hard for her little one.

The lamb is tiny, a *petit bébé,* black and white, the size of a large kitten. She tries to stand, and struggles to her feet, not even stumbling, eyeing her surroundings as though she is quite content in her new world. I have never seen anything so cute, so darling, so inexplicably amazing. Sadness and joy at the same time, like the sun and the rain in a rainbow, the little thing wobbling, my black curly sweetheart. Nothing, I decide, nothing at all, is like a baby lamb. How can there be such innocence in this world?

William Blake refers to lambs in, *Of Innocence* and *Of Experience.* I didn't finish either treatise, because, among other things, I was turned off by all the talk of lambs. But, after scrutinizing this tiny newborn, I know what Blake means. A kitten plays for a while, a puppy tries to please. But a lamb! A lamb wonders and wanders on her thin, wobbly legs, like she is big and brave. This newborn lamb touches a place so deep, it feels ancient, like a place I departed too long ago to even remember. Is that what they call your soul? All I know is, I can't imagine ever eating lamb again.

When it's time to head home, I pick up my little bundle. I'm beaming in the golden sunlight. Across the mountains, a magnificent rainbow of colored mists rises from the sea. Do I believe in signs? If I did, this would be one.

"Randy," I say breathlessly upon entering kitchen, "a baby lamb was born." Randy works behind the kitchen table, sifting flour for an apple cake. He grins. "Did everything go well?"

"Oh yeah—I hardly had to do anything. And the baby is sooooo darling."

It dawns on me—a baby lamb is nothing new for Randy. He lived on a sheep station—the correct word for a sheep farm in Australia—with a thousand sheep. He's watched dozens, if not hundreds, of lambs being born. He asks more questions about the baby and the birth and her mom. Actually helping give birth—there is nothing like it.

One day passes after another without Camilla. I get the children off to school, we all complete our chores, and we resurrect our family life, no longer drenched with grief. "Marie," Jacques says to his daughter on my day off, "you need to do the dishes and sweep the floor." I pretend to read while I watch Marie. Her face puffs out, pink, like she wants to stick out her tongue at her Dad. Instead of washing, she rearranges the dishes, clanging the silverware, making as loud a racket as she can.

That's how I used to be. I used to hate work, and I remember feeling that rankling resentment. While Camilla loves work, Marie despises it. She hasn't done dishes in a month. I'm tempted to do them for her, rather than leaving them on the counter, but Marie needs to do the work herself. "Marie," Jacques says a few hours later, his voice a few octaves lower. "Do the dishes!" A wry smile creeps across my face as she avoids her job, puttering and fiddling with everything but the dishes. When Jacques leaves, I want to say, "Get off your ass!" Instead, I clean my room. That is, I stoop under the eaves to fold my clothes and pile my books nice and tidy. Done. Loft clean.

Below me, I finally hear the clink, clink of Marie washing the dishes. "Marie," I say when I descend. "Nice work. Thanks for doing the dishes." I help her dry, and she wipes her hands, beaming at my appreciation.

Work transforms, creates, brings to life something which didn't exist before: a pie for Randy, leather bells for Jacques, a sparkling kitchen for Marie. Being lazy now seems stupid, wasteful, like throwing life away.

Maurice, a beige and white doe, loiters away from the others the following day, bending her knees, and plummeting to her side, moaning, a horrid, painful cry. "Maurice!" I clutch my hat with two hands, so it won't soar in the wind, and sprint to her. She heaves her stomach, expanding and contracting, "Come on, Maurice." I massage her stomach gently as she moans. My second birth ever, and here I am again, alone on the hillside with my herd.

In her goat sort of way, Maurice grimaces, baring her teeth in pain. "You'll be okay. Push! Just push!" A tiny, glossy head emerges between her legs, and I try to slip my hands up into her vagina and grasp the tiny legs.

Goddamn it, I wouldn't know if everything were right. But this does not look right. Maurice shrieks. Something is wrong. Very wrong. She lifts her head and flops it down, exhausted. Her little *enfant* is stuck, unable to budge backward or forward. Mama marshals all her strength, while I tug as tenderly as I can. She cries a scream that crawls up my spine. I pull some more, and her gooey baby emerges. Limp. Dead.

The winds subside as I pet Maurice's soft fur, her stomach rising and falling like stormy ocean waves. She raises her head, strains to sit, and licks her dead baby and the embryo sack. On and on she licks, crying her lament all afternoon. "Oh, Maurice." I rub her forehead. I know so little about how long she gestated, or what I should do. Was there any other way to help her? Her cry is so mournful, so human. Birth and death at the same time. What does that say about the spirit? Or where it goes? I lift the wet, dead baby, and tuck it in my green canvas bag, leaving the sticky afterbirth behind. For the rest of the afternoon, Maurice trails next to me. At the end of the day, I nestle her in straw in the barn. Jacques removes the dead baby. I never learn where he takes the lifeless bodies.

I describe the scene on the hillside to Randy. His jaw tightens while he taps an egg on a bowl, cracks it, and, tosses the yolk back and forth from one shell to the other, separating it out. "It's not surprising the baby died," he says. "The pregnant goats should never have been exposed to the blizzards and snowstorms. They should have stayed in the barn, warm all winter long." I nod. Poor Maurice and her baby. Dozens of goats are pregnant. What does this death foretell?

Randy folds cheese into beaten egg whites for his omelet. "I think I'll add some parsley," he says, as in 'what do you think?' Not asking for permission, but inviting input, which epitomizes the respect and unspoken affection between us.

"Parsley sounds good," I say. "I'm going to collect more eggs." My anxieties about running the farm were misplaced, in spite of the death of a baby goat. I've developed my routine; I know what to do, and so does Randy. It seems impossible that we don't need Camilla to make it work, but we don't. We really don't.

I return from the chicken coop with four eggs tucked under my sopping-wet coat. "Any mail?"

"I got a letter." Randy pauses before he tells me the news. "My family bought a ticket for me to return to Australia on May 9."

My jaw falls. It's early February, but May 9 seems so soon. Our time together is suddenly finite. The end feels like a brick wall, a wall we'll hit in just a few months. Randy seems like a part of me—so close, so tied to me. And though I'll miss him tremendously, I still don't know what I want from him. Will we always be like brother and sister, the closest of friends, or will we be lovers? My voice sticks in my throat. "May 9," I say.

Another week passes, and again, it's my day off. What should I do? The winds have subsided, the air warmed, and shockingly, the sun hovers overhead. I climb over thyme and sage and rocks to find Randy guarding the goats. Frippo and Natasha bask in the sunshine, while Randy chats to some mama goats, petting their heads. "Want to have a picnic?" I ask.

"Sure."

I skip down the hill, exhilarated by the sunshine, and toss some cheese and bread and wine into a wicker basket, like it's *au naturel* for this city girl to be romping the hills of France.

"*Voici!*" I say, finding a flattish rock on which to sit and eat. I pour some wine into two of our usual fruit glasses, and hand Randy the basket.

"Look at Georgia," Randy says between bites. "She's so big. She might have twins." He opens his army knife and cuts off a piece of cheese. "But I'm more concerned with Scarlett. She lags behind wherever we go."

"With me, too" The black-and-white-spotted doe chews her leaves listlessly. "You know, I miss Camilla," I say.

"But we're really managing quite well," says Randy. Elusive skulks closer, as though we won't notice, pointing her nose toward the picnic basket. Her bell tinkles.

"Yeah. We are," I respond. "She's a great teacher, but we're good students, too. I miss her more as friend than anything else."

Randy eyes Scarlett, ignoring me.

That evening, everyone in the house feels lighter, even chipper. "*Ay liz a bet a,*" Jacques says, "will you cut my hair?"

"*Oui,*" I say. I've never cut hair before and usually Jacques chops off his own hair, but tonight he props himself on the hard chair with shoulders high, his back straight, and a napkin around his neck. Marie, Louis, Randy, and I gather around. Jacques hands me long, silver scissors that look like a garden tool. I start chopping. Vroom! Off to the races! I cut on Jacques' left side, but shit! It's crooked. I try again on the other side to balance it off. Oh, no! I cut some more. And some more. And some more. The scent of the apple cake, just out of the oven wafts from the kitchen. I keep hacking. Now Jacques' hair looks all lopsided, like one of the Three Stooges with a bowl over his head.

The scissors squeak with each whack, and with a bit here, a bit there, I dig myself into a greater and greater disaster, with no help from Louis, Marie, and Randy. They all cover their mouths with their hands to stifle their laughter. Jacques' locks fall off his shoulder onto the floor and finally, we're all laughing outright. Every chop that's meant to improve the hair only makes it worse. We're all hysterical, bowling over. How hard can it be to cut hair for someone like Jacques who doesn't care a bit about his appearance? He rolls his eyes upward, trying to see his own hair, but the only mirror in the house is the tiny rectangle hanging on the nail in the loft, so he can't tell what on earth we're laughing about.

Poor Jacques! His mouth forms a gimpy smile. I stand back, examine my work. What a mess. His hair, which usually looks like a blond stack of hay, is now like a ragged ball of string going every which way. It's horrible. Awful, and yet, so funny. We all double over, holding our tummies, in stitches.

"Randy, do you think I should cut a little more on the right side?" My voice sputters between my laughs, and of course, speaking in English only makes Jacques more uncomfortable. He stiffens, looking straight ahead. Is that a faint trace of a smile?

"Randy, do you want to try?" I ask. Randy steps back, walks first to the left, then to the right, around Jacques.

"Mmm," he finally says, hand to his chin in a pensive manner, as though approaching a chunk of marble to carve The Pieta. "Mmm." Then, ever so carefully, he picks up the shears. Snip, snip, snip, on one side, then snip, snip, on the other. Actually though, there isn't much he can do. Marie brings down the mirror, and Jacques rips the towel from around his neck and takes a look. He grins impishly, shrugs his shoulders and pours his wine. No fashion show for Jacques this spring.

If Jacques hadn't used pruning shears to cut his own hair last time, I might have taken the job more seriously. Even so, I don't think he knew it was possible to butcher his hair quite so badly. But horrible as the haircut is, it seems to unite all of us. There's nothing like a good laugh to connect people, and now we feel more bonded than ever.

Yes, Camilla's absence creates a void. But we fill the void with a sense of joy, absent after Marian's death. I can't tell what Jacques thinks of the haircut, but I doubt he really cares.

As for me, I'm sorry I botched his hair so badly, but I've never been great with my hands. My strengths are, instead, bringing people together, and knowing when to delegate. I find people who are skilled, and let them succeed where I might not.

Out with the goats a day later, a voice startles me from behind a tree. I brush dirt off my butt and stand. "Hey, Randy." I'm glad he's dropped by on his day off. Randy scratches Lucy's head, and rubs his hand across Coconut's full stomach. I smell the mounds of thyme that survived the cold and snow. "Everyone seems to be doing well," he says. "There'll be lots of babies soon." We ramble back down the hills for dinner, discussing our goats like they're our children, laughing as though our lives were carefree. I feel like taking his arm—it seems like the right thing to do—but I don't. We're so happy together. What a change from the darkness we felt just a week ago.

Randy stirs the rabbit stew for noon dinner, even though it's his day off, while I set the table, dinging the silverware in my hand. I read him a letter from Susannah; and Randy reads his letter from his mother and his sister. His sister writes, "Are you going to bring Elizabeth home with you?"

What? She wonders if he's going to bring me home? To Australia? I don't know what I think. It never occurred to me in a million years to go to Australia with him. I'm so confused. Randy means so much to me, but go to Australia? I need to be *super* careful of his feelings.

When *Louisianne* finishes on the radio, I feed the calf, roast chicory coffee, shake the milk 'til it turns to cream, cut veggies for soup, and wash the cheese forms. Jacques disappears to relocate the paddocks for his horses. His passion, the horses, always come first, before the goats, the family, or the rest of the farm. Sure, he needs the goats, sheep, and cow for income. But the horses are his love.

When the whole family assembles once more in the *salle à manger* for supper, we eat in peace. Phew! When Camilla ruled the nest, Louis and Marie constantly fought for her attention. Louis could do nothing wrong, and Marie, nothing right. Camilla was our axis, our director, our decider. Without her, roles have shifted, and yet, the work is all accomplished. We have peace. Funny how that works.

After dinner, Marie, Jacques, and I discuss theories of the universe. "The problems of the world come because the material world is progressing more rapidly than the spiritual world," Jacques says. Fascinating. He thinks there's *communal spiritual progress*, not just *personal spiritual growth*. Could that be true? Are our hearts and souls growing collectively? Little pockets exist around the globe, like here in Languedoc, where people have turned their backs on mainstream society to live more spiritually, closer to Whomever their God may be. And yet, moving back to nature certainly wasn't the answer for Marian. I press my finger to my lips, thinking. The concept of progress in our spiritual world intrigues me.

On Saturday, Louis sets the table for the first time without being asked. "*Louis, merci!*" I say. I feed the calf, milk the cow, take a break for an apple and milk, wash dishes, boil potatoes for dinner, shake the milk jar to make more butter, shift the *fromage* into the next round of forms, set them out on the racks to dry in the *fromagerie*, serve dinner, put away the dishes, and clean the stove by nine o'clock. I am tired; but life is good.

The following day the sunshine turns to rain, and once again we're miserable and cold. Randy and I milk quickly. When we shuffle back to the house with buckets of milk, Marie has cleaned the whole downstairs, and done all the dishes. All without being told! "Marie," I say. "*Merci! Merci!*" We're all growing up together.

Chapter Fourteen

Change

"*Papa*, let's go to the movies," Marie says one night at supper. "Randy and Elizabeth, do you want to go to the movies?" There's a movie theater around here? My mouth drops. How long has it been since I've seen a movie, or a screen of any sort? Eight months at least.

"Yes!" In a heartbeat.

We all drive to the tiny theater, several villages down the road. We purchase tickets, and creep past a heavy velvet curtain to find our seats. As I wait for the film to start, I remember going to the movies with Garner.

A group of six or seven of us went to Monty Python's *Life of Brian* in the theater in Eugene. We loved the intensity of the front row when we ate acid, so we settled in with our salty popcorn. Plus, with Garner's bad eyes—he refused to get glasses—he could actually see the movie. The theater smelled of butter as the lights dimmed, the screen lit up, and the show began. Right from the beginning, we roared with laughter. Tears rolled off my cheeks. In the middle of the movie, Garner squeezed by to go to the restroom. I pulled in my knees, swiveled my head around so not to miss a word of the movie. Each scene was hysterical. I forgot all about my popcorn. Caught up in the movie, I forgot about Garner, too. "Where is he?" Susannah whispered.

Yeah, he had been gone awhile. Just then he appeared, landed on his seat, and clutched my hand. As the reds and greens of the movie screen glowed on his face, I knew something was wrong.

"I went into the wrong movie," he whispered.

Later, in the lobby, he said, "Yeah, man. I came back to the movie after going to the head, and I go in, and I'm sittin' there waiting for Monty Python, and here comes Robert de Niro." The pinball machine in the lobby pinged behind us. "It was a war! Vietnam! All that jungle and creepy bugs and snakes and then de Niro pulls this fuckin head out a cage. A cage! Like a birdcage." Garner jumped in place as he told his story, totally freaked out. "Oh, shit, I thought. This ain't no *Life of Brian.* I hightailed it out of there."

Only crazy Garner could walk into *Apocalypse Now* when he's looking for *Monty Python.*

I chuckle to myself in the tiny theater in France. Yep, that's Garner. That guy I'm done with.

I sit between Randy and Marie, waiting for the lights to dim. Suddenly, guns blast as cowboys tear across the screen, riding their mahogany steeds past cacti, through the desert, in *El Condor,* a decade-old American western with no famous movie stars and dubbed over in French. I only catch bits and pieces of the speedy dialogue. French dialogue, made in Hollywood, set in Mexico. How could life get better?

"Hey, Randy," I say a few days later. "You know, that's quite a mess in front of the house. You know all those chunks of concrete in between the front and the road? It sure would be nice if all that crap were gone."

"What are you talking about?"

"It looks like a dump." The door opens and Jacques stomps the mud off his boots. "Jacques, what do you think about cleaning up those chunks of concrete in front of the house?"

Soon enough, Randy and Jacques grab some shovels and away they go, digging through the chunky piles. I make the *fromage de chevre*, and just as I finish the last mound, Randy returns. "Come see."

The air smells fresh, with wild poppies budding. Jacques and Randy lean on their shovels, smiling in pride at the cleared area in front of the house. "*Magnifique*!" I say. "*C'est beau*!" What a difference an hour of shoveling can make!

"Ay liz a bet a et Rand-ee," Jacques says later that afternoon, "The children and I are going to the grandparents for supper." An hour later, Marie calls, "*À toute à l'heure* ."

I feel a tingling I've denied. For weeks. For months. Randy and I eat our supper in front of the hissing fire, and the electric sparks I've tried to bury spread throughout my body. We savor our soup, our bread, and of course, our wine.

Washing the dishes, Randy hums, saying little. There's nothing unusual about Randy humming. He often hums. But tonight is different. There's energy in the room, an energy between us that I believe we both can feel. I snap open the cassette player and play Cat Stevens, *Tea for the Tillerman.* I glace at Randy from the corner of my eye. Randy, the petit boy with blond hair, the boy I spend day and night with, day after day, week after week, the boy who knows my every nuance, my every gesture, but not my body. We've never touched, as though we're covered in thin coats, protected, shielded.

I chew on my pen, not writing in my journal, and I feel my body flush. I wipe my brow, I feel my breasts rise, moisture between my legs. Will tonight be the night?

"Do you want to plan our trip?" he asks. With the fire snapping, the smoke smells sweet.

"Sure."

We huddle together, perusing Louis' photo books on the Danube, the Swiss Alps, and Italy. I'm dying to ask the sort of questions I discuss with Jacques and Marie. I rest my head on my elbow and ask, "Randy, does it make sense to talk about 'a secret of the universe? Do you think there's a 'spiritual way,' not just a material plane?" I'm losing him, but I continue. "Does prayer make any sense to you?"

Oops! How to kill a moment.

He tilts his head, and says, "I haven't thought about those questions and really, I could care less."

Whoa! I raise my eyebrows. Could care less? Not the sort of response that leads to intimacy. The one person I can talk to in English, my very best friend in this tiny universe, sees life so differently than I do.

"*Bonjourrrr. Hallooo.*" A visitor saves us, the intense, awkward moment. Teresa, an English girl, peeks her head in. "Hello. My name is Teresa. The headlight on my motor bike went out," she says.

"Come in, come in." Randy and I both stand. "Take a spot by the fireplace to warm up. Wine?" We've never met Teresa, but that's the neighborly way of this remote mountain road. If a stranger comes to the door, we welcome them with open arms.

I sometimes feel like Randy and I live on a desert island and Randy is way too good for me—so pure. I just want to raise hell once in awhile. The moment of closeness, near intimacy, is gone. Vanished. Randy slides down to the other end of the table to study his stamps, while Teresa and I drink our wine, chat, laugh. Later, I wonder, am I falling for Randy, or am I leading him on? I feel confused; that's all I know.

The following morning, I mend a stack of clothes as Randy herds in the rain. My stitches are now straight, small, even. Precise, gorgeous, fit for a queen. Or even Camilla. In the afternoon, I herd the goats in a rainstorm. I'm drenched. Heaven is being dry in the evening.

"Let's plan our trip," I say to Randy after evening supper. "We can pick up where we left off last night. I have about $1,100 American dollars, but I'd like to save around $500 for getting resettled when I go home to America."

"Well, I have what comes to about $4,000 American dollars. Let's just put our money together."

John Prine twangs on the cassette player, *Grandpa was a carpenter*. "Randy, no, I can't do that."

"Why not?"

"Well, I can't borrow money like that. I won't." Randy blinks as though he feels hurt. "No, Randy. Please. Don't even think about it. I don't know how long it will take me to get a job when I get home, or how long it would take to pay it back." His eyes narrow. "Really, thanks." I try to reassure him. "Let's just plan our trip so we each spend the same amount of money. If we hitchhike and stay in hostels, eat bread and cheese and wine—so much cheaper than bottled water—we'll be okay."

He agrees, with reluctance.

"So, do you want to start with Morocco? I'm dying for some sun and heat."

"Morocco?" Jacques pipes in. "You should go there! The people are poor, but they're very, very spiritual. Islamic countries are usually more spiritual than Christian countries."

Mmm. Interesting perspective. I know that women wear veils all the time, and can't go out to places where the men drink their tea, so things can't be so great for them. Jacques thinks more highly of Russia than the United States, which seems so bizarre to me. Both are run by the mafia, according to Jacques, as well as by the rich oil companies.

I glance at Randy and see in his eyes how important I am to him. I'm touched by his kindness in offering to pay for me. After having been fat and feeling ugly for so many years, it's still hard to accept that men are attracted to me. When I visited London before I went to Paris, I met a man,

Peter, who showed me London from the point of view of a native. He drove me to where bombed buildings from World War II still stood hollowed out, as though they were pulverized yesterday. "This is what happened because it took you so long to enter the war," he said. I cried. He hugged me. Three days later, he waited with me at the station before I headed first to Dover, and then on to Paris. The bus chugged in, its brakes screeched, and I threw my backpack over my shoulder. "Stay here," he pleaded. "Stay with me in London." Of course I wouldn't stay. Paris called! When I boarded my bus, he waved with tears in his eyes, saying, "You're going to go all over Europe, breaking hearts!" I had dismissed Peter's words. Me, the unattractive woman who no one invited to a single dance or prom? No man ever talked to me like that! It felt vain to even think it.

And yet, I've changed. It's true. And with that change, comes a new force in my life—men's attraction to me. I need to approach men and relationships differently, Men have feelings, too. A strange new concept.

Now, sitting with Randy and Jacques in the *salle à manger* , planning the next step of my European—maybe African—adventure—I accept that I'm a different woman than I was. More than slender, I'm confident and comfortable, and I believe in myself. I need to remember Randy is *très timide* with other people. Perhaps, he has no friends besides me and his broken family. Could that be true? Sometimes he acts like he doesn't need anyone, but of course he does. And perhaps those few people he brings into his life, like me, mean much more than I imagined.

When we're alone, Randy and I laugh and joke. He's the genius of the farm who reminds me of the blind goatherd in the children's adventure book, *The Secret of Killimooin,* who says *"I am no good in a strange place. My feet, my ears, my hands only help me when I am on my mountain-side. In a strange place, I am lost."* Randy, too, might be lost outside the farm.

While I, the city girl, hitchhiked alone all over America, Canada, and France; Randy rarely left his Australia farm before he came to the Fontaines. He's never hitchhiked. Yes, Randy is *petit* and fragile, but together we'll be okay.

Randy's birthday is a few days away, and I want to make it special. What does he love the most? The goats, certainly. Suddenly, light bulb! I'll collect nuts that he can give to the goats. I'll stuff my pockets with handfuls every day. The perfect present. It won't be easy, with snow and mud covering most of the nuts, but having treats to give the herd will thrill him.

"Marie," I say, taking her aside, "Want to help me decorate a birthday cake for Randy?"

"*Ah, oui,*" she says, her smile brightening. We bake the cake while Randy is herding. Then begins the fun, the art of frosting. We mix powdered sugar with our homemade butter and separate the batch in two, adding powered chocolate to half. After that, we dip a slender knife in the frosting and twirl the white and chocolate, curling little flowers along the edges of the top. Marie writes "Randy" in script in the middle. I design the edges. I start to add more decorations when Marie rests her hand on mine. "*Non. Non.*" she says. "*C'est fini.* No, that's enough."

She's right. "*Oui*" Enough! The cake is beautiful. Americans tend toward excess, to overdo; but the French know beauty, know when enough is perfect.

Randy's birthday falls on my day off. I nudge Marie. "Wake up. It's time." I light the fire, and we arrange a tray with coffee, toast, butter, jam, and even a twig of thyme in a glass like a flower in a vase. "*Prêt?*" I ask Marie. "Ready?"

We pull back the curtain to the boys' sleeping area. "*Bonjour,* Randy," Marie and I say in unison, handing him his breakfast. "*Joyeux anniversaire!*" Randy smiles slightly, as though he doesn't know how to react. "Happy Birthday," I say, handing him the bag of nuts for the goats as well as the gloves my Mom had mailed me. The dripping butter on the bread we toasted on a stick over the fire smells sweet. Jacques appears from behind the curtain and gives Randy a belt he made.

I've heard about people who are at "a loss for words," but I've never seen it like this. Randy examines the belt with its shiny silver buckle, the nuts, and the gloves, until words dribble from his mouth, "Thank you." Marie and I laugh, happy to score a home run on this birthday surprise.

"Randy, you don't need to take the goats out this afternoon," Jacques says. "I'll watch them." Randy blinks. Jacques has never taken out the herd, except with us, and then only to show us new routes. Is this another birthday present from Jacques? Randy having the day off, so we can be together?

Randy asks me if I'd like to see some ruins he discovered. "*Bien sûr.*" Sure. I love exploring. We climb up and down the hills, exploring caves, ancient deserted houses, and falling ruins. After supper Marie and I light the thick candle we use for reading, center it on the cake, and Marie turns off the lone kitchen light bulb. I carry the birthday cake to Randy. It isn't perfect. The frosting could use more vanilla, but, thanks to Marie's touches, it's beautiful. On our coaxing, Randy makes a wish and blows it out. When he cuts pieces for us all, we stick our fingers in the frosting and lick them clean. Yum! It's not the idea that counts, I decide. It's the love put into it. And I put so much love—some kind of love—into Randy's birthday.

When I awaken in the morning, I feel like I remember an ancient truth I once knew. When people truly find "it," *a true spiritual connection*, they don't gloat or advertise it with bumper stickers about Jesus. They share it, give it away, often silently, humbly. "It" is giving, sharing, loving. That's how I feel the morning after Randy's birthday.

At breakfast, the radio drones, white noise, and I feel especially calm and serene until Jacques bursts into the *salle à manger*. *"Ay liz a bet a,"* he says, sounding urgent, "take the goats out, be sure to include Mistral (the horse), the baby lamb, and her mother, and Rusty." (Rusty's the one with a cast). I'm taken aback. Before I can herd, I need to start dinner and milk the cow all by myself. Jacques trots off to move the portable electric fences for the horses, always his first priority. I longed for a moment to drink my chicory and wake up.

The crusty snow cracks under my boots as I wonder how I'll herd forty goats, twelve sheep, a cow, a calf, a horse, a goat with a broken leg, and a baby lamb. With two hands, I push open the heavy barn door and search hopelessly for a rope. "I'm so mad!" I scream to the cows and the goats and sheep. "How am I supposed to tie the horse, loop the rope around his mouth and neck, and lead all the animals up the mountain, when I don't where the cord is? Is it common sense to know how to do all this?"

I march back to the house, pound my foot, and yell at Randy, so furious that something sticks in my throat. Am I this angry because Jacques disturbed my peaceful breakfast? Suddenly, everything is rush, rush, rush. Or is it my hormones? Too much wine last night? Randy, washing the forms, glances at my hands on my hips and laughs at me. With me.

"You want some help?" he asks,\ with sympathy. I rarely show my anger like this. In the past, I ate instead. Afraid? Mad? Worried? Food was the answer. But here on the farm, where I've awakened in the past to Camilla and Marie screaming, to Jacques and Michel yelling, and to Marie and Louis fighting, no feelings are hidden. Oddly, I feel more centered than I ever have, even in my rage.

"Here's the cord," he says, pulling it out from behind a bale of hay in the barn. He helps tie it around the horse's head.

"Okay, guys. Frippo, Natasha. *Allez, Allez,*" I say, as my little tribe and I exit the barn.

"Good luck!" Randy says, waving, as he turns back to finish his chores. The horse is the same stubborn, old, troublemaker I tried to ride three times. What a sight, the five of us: a horse, the little goat with her broken leg, the mama sheep, and the lamb, all trailing behind fifty other animals. Finally, I laugh at myself as I round the bend and the house vanishes from view.

"Ay liz a bet a." Marie calls to me in the *fromagerie* where I'm setting out a dozen mounds of goat cheese to dry. "Your mom is on the phone."

After the small talk about the family, my Mom clears her throat and states the true reason for her call. "What exactly are your travel plans?" I hear an edge, worry in her voice.

"Well, Randy and I will travel from here to Madrid, across the straits of Gibraltar to Morocco, and after that, we're not sure. Maybe Rome, maybe Paris. Then, back to the farm. Randy leaves for Australia May 9."

"Do you really think that's a good idea? Going to Northern Africa?"

Talk about a loaded question. I bristle. "Mom, we'll be fine!" I'm pissed that after all this time, my mom questions my plans, and yet, I regret reacting so. My mom and I hang up.

Actually, I do wonder about traveling with Randy. Sometimes he bugs me, but mostly, we get along beautifully. He's changing, criticizing Jacques far less frequently. After so many years of being judgmental, he must still have his nit-picking thoughts, but now he doesn't spout them quite so often.

Chapter Fifteen
Homecoming

Camilla's finally coming home! We're each excited in our own way. Marie and Louis miss their mom. Maybe, Jacques anticipates lessening his workload as much as seeing his wife. And I'm ready to relinquish all my extra duties—planning menus, caring for the children, tending all the babies and the pregnant mamas.

The final morning before her return, I milk the cow, feed the goats, gather eggs, wash towels, and begin cooking dinner. Mr. Bawdy bursts in the kitchen. "*Mademoiselle,*" he yells—he doesn't know how to speak in a normal voice—"*Mademoiselle, Ay liz a bet a, Tu es une bonne ménagère*
Tu es une bonne ménagère!" You are a good housewife!

A good housewife? What? A good June Cleaver? *Please!* A housewife was the *last* thing I ever wanted to be. Me? The adventurer, the explorer, the wanderer? But it's true. I performed Camilla's job well, tending to the work, the kids, the goats, the sheep, Ma Rosa, her baby, the farm, and the house. *Une bonne ménagère,* indeed.

I traipse out to feed the rabbit, nodding to Randy who's washing the forms. "Be back in a minute." My fears and anxieties about Camilla's absence had been unfounded.

Now, I am truly responsible. It's not an act, a performance. People honestly do change, and Randy and I run the farm and manage the children quite well.

Waiting for Camilla after supper, Jacques leafs through his coffee table book with photos of Camargues. These majestic and graceful beasts, he explains, descended from the extinct *Soutré* horse, whose bones date from 17,000 years ago. Seventeen thousand years! I can't imagine. Jacques' face radiates as he elucidates about the horses—their history, their strengths, their beauty. He drifts into another world when he points to their boxy noses and strong haunches. It's as though the photos themselves breathe within this book.

The twigs in the fire snap and a small, blue flame flickers over the burning embers. We begin to yawn. First Louis, then Randy, then Jacques, say, "*Bonne nuit.*" Only Marie stays up, hoping to see her mother.

I sleep well that night. Camilla will be home and life will return to normal. But on her very first morning home, I wake to angry voices. The words are fuzzy, but the tones, familiar. Camilla has been home only a few hours and she and Marie are already fighting. During Camilla's absence, Marie called her and sent her a card. She missed her mom tremendously, and spoke of her often. But, even though Camilla loves Marie, she doesn't seem to like her very much.

Camilla always favors Louis. In Camilla's absence, Marie and Jacques forged an alliance, a bond that evaporates with Camilla's homecoming. With her return, the power's shifted back. No matter what Camilla and Marie fought about this morning, the underlying emotions are clear. Marie resents that Camilla doesn't show her a bit of affection. Marie envies Louis. Camilla yells at Marie for things Louis can get away with. Marie vies for attention by using baby talk, asking stupid questions, annoying her mom and everyone else. When her Mom dotes on her brother, Marie retaliates by screaming at both Camilla and Louis. Now, she slams the door on her way to the school bus.

I step into the kitchen where Camilla, dressed in her familiar blue apron, stirs the stew in front of the wood stove, her tortoise shell glasses slipping down her nose. "Welcome home! You had a good trip?" She nods, kisses my cheeks enthusiastically as though she missed me too, and continues to stir. Where she went, or what she did, I never figure out. She rifles through the trash, then dusts, scrubs, and polishes as never before. Yes, Camilla and her tornado-like energy are home.

At noon dinner, Randy rests his fork on his plate with an expressionless face. "*Excuse moi,*" he says. He bolts from the dinner table, leaving his half-eaten stew.

"*Excuse moi,*" I say to Camilla and Jacques, and scurry to catch up as Randy lurches open the barn door. "Randy, what…?" Sounds of crying echo through the musty barn. I trail Randy to the back, where Grand Marnier, one of Randy's favorite goats, wails wretchedly. Her stomach rises and falls in painful breaths.

Jacques follows behind me. "Grand Marnier?" Randy intuitively knew she was in trouble birthing. Grand Marnier lifts her head and drops it. One of the baby's feet catches inside her, but the head has emerged, and he breathes.

Jacques and I hold Grand Marnier down, stroking her neck and back, soothing her, while Randy bends over and pulls. Finally, the *chevreau,* a baby male goat, appears. All of him. Alive.

I'm amazed that I, the city girl, who barely knew a sheep from a goat, I am delivering goats. As Michel, the older brother whom we haven't seen for a month, used to say, "*Incroyable.*" The darling little *chevreau* wobbles, falls, and tries again. The miracle of birth strikes me as just that: a miracle. Randy, Jacques, and I all glow in satisfaction as we watch the tiny, beautiful creature.

Jacques and Randy troop up from the barn to the house, and I unleash the partitions, preparing to guide the herd. My gang and I mosey up the mountain, under the turquoise sky, soft against the surrounding hills, a patchwork of green and brown. Muted sounds of pain stop me. I glance, then charge toward the house. "Jacques! Randy!" I say. "*Depeche! Depeche*!"

Hairy Harrison, who's been losing her way lately, moans grotesquely. Jacques and Randy dash back to the barn, cheeks pink from the cold. Jacques kneels next to Hairy. Randy squats, rubbing her gently, his blond bangs tumbling over his forehead. "There, there, Hairy Harrison." Jacques rolls up his sleeves. He focuses on Harrison's vagina where the little hoofs stick out, but they're stuck. Jacques reaches in his rough fingers as gently as he can, while I pat her face, and yet she still whimpers in agony. Randy rubs her tummy. "It will be over soon," he says.

Yesterday morning Hairy Harrison lagged behind the herd, placing each hoof on the path gingerly, protecting the precious cargo she carried in her womb. Now, as she tries to birth, the other goats and sheep shuffle, breaking the silence in the barn. "*Viens,*" Jacques urges the baby. "Come!" He extends his hands up inside Hairy Harrison to the *petit* knees, and, bit by bit, the hooves appear. Slowly, Jacques pulls again, and soon, all the legs are free. One more tug, and the tummy of the baby emerges.

The other goats in the barn stand still, at attention, sensing the danger. A single bell tinkles. Jacques frowns at Randy, then draws the body a little further. Once more, Hairy Harrison pushes. Jacques tugs again, and finally a tiny head slips out from the exhausted mother. The little *chevrette*, brown and saturated with goo, is the size of a terrier, delicate and sweet. But, her life lasts only moments. The sac covered her face and mouth too long. She smothered. We weren't fast enough. Blood and placenta drip from Jacques' arms up to his elbows, as we all sit in silence, staring at the lifeless body.

I cherish the goats, yet I kill them. I feed chickens, yet I pluck them. I watch the rabbits and yet, I eat them. Surely, I should be used to this cycle of life and death. Still, the sight of this tiny body saddens me. The mama, who tried so hard, flings her head up and drops it to the ground as her breaths deepen. The goats around us coo, restless. Jacques gathers the body of the *chevrette* and exits the barn.

At the end of the day, after evening supper, I bring hot chocolate to the *salle à manger*. Jacques removes an envelope from a drawer in the bureau. "*Voila,*" he says. "Here are some pictures of me in Algeria, during the war." Perhaps twenty years old in the black-and-white photos, Jacques poses in front of a tank with several other soldiers.

"I didn't know you were a soldier," I say. I don't know anything about the French-Algerian war. I later learn that the French Colony of Algeria fought for independence in a war that led to nearly one million deaths. The war raged between 1954 and 1962 with differing loyalties inside Algeria adding complications, and eventually a civil war ravished the country

I'm surprised. Jacques in a war? He draws in his cheeks and straightens his mouth as we examine the photos. Maybe they dredge up memories he'd rather forget. And yet, he's revealing them to me and I am honored.

In one photo, Jacques stands in front of a crumbling concrete home with a group of men wearing French uniforms holding their guns. Jacques hadn't wanted to fight, he said. Algeria was France's Vietnam, I think. Of course, Vietnam was France's Vietnam, as well.

We return to the atlas, where Jacques suggests places for Randy and me to travel. While we discuss Morocco, I think about Bob Dylan's record, *Blood on the Tracks*, an album Garner and I listened to together all the time. Dylan sings, "If you see her, say 'hello,' she may be in Tangiers."

Bob Dylan once obsessed me, especially in college. In fact, on my first cross-country trip when I traveled from the east coast to Oregon with two college friends, I insisted we detour to Dylan's hometown of Hibbings, Minnesota. I found his childhood home and danced around it like an excited girl at a carnival. Before we left town, we cashed travelers' checks at a local bank. When I explained my literary pilgrimage to see Dylan's birthplace, the bank teller scoffed. "Oh, well," he said, "Bob's brother, David, was the real musician. He quit the Minneapolis symphony to be Dylan's manager."

My obsession with Dylan led me to study all his songs, albums, every biography, and all his influences. Rimbaud and Baudelaire influenced Dylan, so I read Rimbaud and Baudelaire. They'd been influenced by Blake, so I read Blake. Or, at least, I tried.

Maybe I'll send Garner a postcard from Tangiers, Morocco, with a drawing of tracks in red, like *Blood on the Tracks.* Just when I think Garner's out of my head, he pops up once more.

"Do you want to go to Algeria and Tunisia after Morocco?" I ask Randy, sipping my hot chocolate. "I mean, it would be fun. Fascinating. But, they're really far." We refer to the atlas. "About 2,000 kilometers. That's a long way across a desert."

The phone sounds its piercing ring, breaking our thoughts. Jacques answers.

"*Ay liz a bet a.*"

"Hello," I say.

"Hello," says the French-Australian accent, sharp and unpleasant. Randy's mother's friend, the sixty-five-year-old woman who brought Randy to the farm so long ago, barks at me. "Randy is a very young boy, stupid, and cannot be counted on in an emergency." How rude! "Morocco is filled with thieves. Don't ever leave your bags in your rooms or take your money off your body." The advice on Morocco travel may be helpful, but her arrogant tone exasperates me.

"Of course, I'll take care of Randy," I say. I don't say, "What do you think I'm going to do? Leave him in the markets of Marrakesh?"

Randy shakes his head and pinches his lip, catching the drift of the conversation. He gawps at me for a moment and returns to the map, tracing his fingers across Northern Africa. Frippo, who lies by our feet, snores and flops his head like in a bad dream.

I hang up the phone. "Another one who's not in favor of our travels."

"I could care less what she thinks," Randy says.

Okay, then! "We can hitchhike through France and Spain, and from there, ride a ferry across the Straits of Gibraltar to get to Morocco." We don't ask if we'll need visas. "Once we're in Morocco, I'm not sure where we'll cross to Tunisia and Algeria." Since Michel hitchhiked to Tunisia, or so I understand, there must be a way.

I yearn to see nomads with camels and cliff dwellers. Still, with our budget? It will be hard to fit it all in. Neither Randy nor I have seen the Alps or Germany or Rome or Florence. And, I'd love to visit Paris again. We can't do it all. "We'll save money sleeping in fields and under bridges," I say. "Are you game?"

Randy nods, not raising any objections. I'll find out soon enough how much of an adventurer he really is.

Randy and I tell Camilla and Jacques our departure date: March 15. Jacques says before we go, he'll take us sightseeing.

Sightseeing? I have no idea what we'll see, but I wash with my sponge bath the night before and dress in my fresh, non-farm clothes, feeling crystal clean. I think we've all worn the same clothes for a month. We probably stink to the outside world. Since we only leave the farm at most once a month, does that make us hermits? Stinking hermits? I'm glad to dress in the clean jeans I packed away, my clean turtleneck, and the lovely, but not warm enough, jacket my mom sent.

We drive off to Beziers, then head southwest to *Oppidum d'Enserune.* Excavations reveal that a Celtic town thrived here on a hilltop between 6th century BC and 1st century AD. I can't fathom that! We can actually see the foundation of the ancient city where eight thousand people once lived. Next to that, we note the current museum with silos, funeral urns, and Greek pottery, believed to have been traded thousands of years ago by the Greeks. Fascinating as it may be, and it truly is, my main joy is hanging out with Randy, off on an adventure. Through all the ups and downs in my emotions, I love being near him, with him. What an important friend! Frankly, being together distracts me from the wonder of the site.

Two days later, Jacques, Randy, and I leave in darkness and head west before we turn south. I sleep soundly until Jacques nudges me. "*Ay liz a bet a, voila!*" The sun rises from behind the mountain, as bright as a red poppy. Poised on the hill, a magnificent castle rises before us. I sit up straighter and press my forehead to the windshield. A real, live castle! And we're not at Disneyland! I squint and twist my head, stretching my neck to see as much as I can: broad turrets, stone walls, even a drawbridge.

"Randy, Randy!" I say. "Look. Just like in fairy tales and nursery rhymes." Cinderella, Sleeping Beauty, Rapunzel... And now, reality. The castle is Carcassonne, one of the oldest walled cities in all of Europe. Within Carcassonne lies *La Cité,* the ancient walled city built by the early Romans. Some of their original walls remain.

We park and hustle inside, where we face the gift shop. "Just a sec. I'll buy some guidebooks." I leaf through the racks and, no surprise, all the guide books are written in France. I decide on Michelin's book on Europe, another on travel in Africa, and finally, a guide to Carcassonne. With my flawed French, I'm a bit challenged, but these should help. In the meantime, Jacques buys tickets for us for the French tour of *La Cité.*

During the thirteenth century, I gather, the anti-Cather crusaders used Carcassonne as their base for murder and torture. By the end of the thirteenth century, Saint Louis IX besieged the fortress and his son strengthened the ramparts, giving it its present look. A century ago, the state commissioned its repair, and rebuilt the cathedral, turrets and towers. That's why we were greeted by such an authentic looking castle—years of restoration.

We meander toward the dungeon, hearing only French, as I expected. But out of the crowds of tourists, I hear English. American English, no less. Yay! The last American I spoke to in English—outside of phone calls—was my cousin, and seven months have passed since then. "Hi," I say to a young couple in their twenties, dressed in jeans and tee shirts. I start speaking rapidly. "I've lived here in France and you're the first Americans I've spoken to in seven months." My heart pounds. "It's sooo wonderful to speak to an American," I plunge on. "Where are you from? Are you here on vacation? Here for long?"

They speak in a monotone, my excitement clearly not reciprocated. The undercurrent: *Hey, we're on our vacation in Europe. We're not interested in someone from America.* "Eugene," they say in dull voices. "Eugene, Oregon. Or, that's where we live now. We go to the University of Oregon."

"Eugene? Really?" Now, I'm popping out of my shoes. "That's where I'm from! At least that's where I lived last!" I can't talk fast enough. "I went to U of O, too. I can't believe it!"

Before I can continue, the tall man says, "Cool," loops his arm around the woman, and wanders in the opposite direction. I'm ready to chase after them, waving my arms. Oregon? You're from Eugene? Don't you want to talk to me?

I remain still. They fade from sight. Oh, well. Maybe after all these months living in the mountains, I'm more connected to Randy and Jacques than these traveling Oregonians.

Chapter Sixteen

Babies

Randy and I check on the pregnant goats every evening. The day after Carcassonne, another set of twins is born. And the following day, just before noon dinner, a new *chevreau,* a baby boy. Elusive's daughter scampers and jumps when she's a few days old. So darling. The baby goats are like my children.

On the one hand, many babies die, either at birth or after living only a day or two.. With so many little *chevreau* and *chevrettes*, and so many pregnant moms, we need to check in the barn every night to ensure everyone is alright. I've come to eagerly anticipate these evenings when Randy and I stroll down to the barn under the black sky with the stars, twinkling like fireflies. Our physical contact is still zilch.

Another day, another climb to the hills with my tribe. In the afternoon, I birth a goat, all by myself, just me and the mama. And she lives. I'm ecstatic about delivering—reaching my hand in, up into the uterus to the baby's body, touching the legs, and finally, to the little head, with its tongue out of its teeny mouth. I gently pull the wet and sticky *petit* chevrette into our world. I don't know the small Mother well, so I call her and the other tiny pregnant goats, "my teenage angels."

After dinner the following afternoon, another *chevre* starts to deliver. "You take out the herd," Jacques says to me. "Randy and I'll take care of her." I glance over my shoulder as I hike up the hill. I hear muffled sounds, but can't distinguish if they're the cries of a healthy birth or not. When I reach the top of the hill, Jacques treks after me to say the *chevre* lived. What an act of kindness for Jacques to clamber up the hill to tell me that both the daughter and mother survived. I feel so grateful. For really, what is happiness but gratitude?

As we start counting the days before we leave, the babies keep coming and coming. Eight births in one day. Yes, *eight.* All of us help.

In the evening, I gaze around the *salle à manger*—Jacques with his books, Louis and Marie with their homework, Camilla with her embroidery. Michel, back home in time for our departure, listens to the Rolling Stones. I love each one, my adopted family, and I'll miss them. And yet, it's time to move on.

In the morning fog layers around me like a silver veil, beyond which a few goats' bells chime. Back at the barn, Randy reports that Pasty White's daughter, just one day old, nearly died. She probably hasn't drunk all day. We try to give her bottled milk, which she resists. That's all we can do.

On Randy's day off, I am supposed to get the babies to drink *away* from their mamas. That means, feeding the tiny ones from a contraption that looks like a tin can with nipples around the bottom. I love to cuddle the little ones, so darling, so soft, so warm. But they object to this drinking device. Sometimes, they don't know how to drink and I try to assist. Sometimes, they just plain rebel. Three times I try. No, they want their mamas' milk. But, we want their mamas' milk, too.

"We're going to have a party," Camilla tells me. She bubbles when she plans parties, and this *mini fête* will be for our departure. Sounds fun to me.

Randy arrives home from his afternoon with the goats earlier than usual. "Look at these guys. They're going to have their babies soon, so I came home early." Awhile later, I rove back to the barn.

"Come on. It's a party for us."

"No. These two are going to birth any minute. And you know how many haven't made it."

"Okay," I say. I'm caught between Camilla who's planned a treat for us and Randy, who's dedicated to the goats. I join Camilla and the party. We all drink Muscat, and on my second glass, Camilla asks, "Where's Randy?"

I slog down to the barn in the foggy rain, slightly tipsy from the Muscat, with mixed emotions. I want to enjoy the *fête* and feel mad that Randy is so good. He prefers to be in the barn with his goats. I also love him for just the same reasons that I'm mad at him—for loving the animals and taking such good care of them. I'm reminded of Levin in *Anna Karenina.*

I open the barn, and know there's trouble. The baby seems to be crying inside the mother, and Randy worries she'll smother. I hold the mother, and he pulls her out.

How many births have been like this, him pulling and me holding? The little ball of fur, drenched in amniotic fluid, walks around his mama. Randy saved another life. And I helped.

For the hundredth time, we trudge from the barn to the house for dinner. After dessert, before coffee, Randy leaves again, and again births another *chevreau.* Before bed, we perform our routine check once more. Jam, who already birthed one baby, has another stuck inside her. Bent backward, the baby is dead by the time we pull him out. Randy leaves to wash his hands, and Jam begins contracting again. I hold the flashlight while Randy helps Jam with yet another baby. She lives. Phew.

We're supposed to start our journey in a few days. After seven months on the farm, I'm traveling to Spain, where a bloodless coup just occurred, to Morocco which is partially at war, and to Algeria and Italy where earthquakes rocked the countries. The new hire, who will replace Randy and me, telephoned to postpone her start date. Again. This is the second time. I'm truly ready to leave.

Pasty's daughter dies. My tears fall.

"*Ay liz a bet a,*" Jacques says, "We're eating dinner at my parents." We, meaning the Fontaine family.

"*À toute à l'heure* "

Randy and I sip our dinner soup. I add extra wood, an extravagance about which I feel only slightly guilty. The flames leap in red and orange and yellow as we discuss shy Elusive, who's getting braver, and Lucy, who's expanding like she's going to have twins. We're hiding behind our words. My heart beats louder, and I wonder if I'll surrender to my aching lust, if we'll pick up where we didn't go the last time.

My gaze sets on his fair skin, his blond locks, his deft hands, and I imagine them touching me, rubbing me, discovering me. Randy, my little shepherd boy and I, the older, experienced woman; I could teach him about love and lust and body fever. The electricity between us ignites. I feel warm, as though my body glows. We laugh. We so often laugh. Two worlds revolve around each other—the one here in a stone room in the South of France, and the one that seethes inside our bodies, ready to burst forth. I can't stand it anymore. I smell the sweet oak of the logs, and just as I'm about to move, it's as though he reads my thoughts—he always can, as though we're of one mind—he disappears up to his loft.

I clear the table and return to the fire. His steps click down the ladder, his slippers clap on the cement, and he enters from the kitchen. He sashays to the fireplace with his hair combed, slicked back, and he rests his elbow on the mantle like Clint Eastwood, like he's "cool," ready to be taken. Who is this boy? He's acting like he's someone else, someone he observed in a movie, someone he never will be. Abruptly, slam, a curtain inside me falls, a door smashes shut, the steam fizzles. Why did he have to comb his hair, slick it back, pose like a stupid movie star? Someone who isn't him at all? He created the exact opposite effect from the one he wanted. Suddenly, Randy isn't the darling young man with the tussled hair, the sweet features, who's waiting to be taken. Now he's a child, a youngster, a young Australian farm boy; a boy who loves his stamps, his goats, his budgies; a fragile boy, a breakable boy, a boy who's trying to act cool. A boy whom I must not hurt.

He remains against the mantel. Flames dart behind him. His eyes fix on mine, penetrating, and my frustration explodes in confusion. He's ruined the moment and I'm pissed. Why do *I* need to be the grown up; the one who faces reality? He shifts his arm, his body, away from the mantel, and he resumes his everyday stance: his back to the fire, his hands clasped behind him. He's nervous, I can tell, by his feigned nonchalance. His slipper falls from his foot, and he reaches his toe to draw it back to him, almost coyly.

"You lost your slipper," I say. My voice is sharp, unwelcoming. In our wordless world, I communicated I wanted one thing: that I wanted to merge our steaming bodies like we did our hearts and souls. I ache for it, and I pity myself for missing out.

I rise to a higher ground. No, I won't take advantage of this gentle boy-man. So it must be. That which I want, that which I crave, will destroy our friendship at best, destroy his thin faith in humanity at worst. Fun for me might spell disaster for him.

I carry my journal and pen to the ladder. "Goodnight," I say. No, I think. I won't spoil his innocence.

The sun shines for the first time in days. But isn't that the story of life on the farm? Rain and sun, laughter and sadness, birth and death, acceptance and letting go? I've gained friendships: friendships with a family and with a boy who, at first glance, seemed as different from me as anyone could be. But we've learned and grown from each other, and now, I'm no longer a city girl. In fact, I wonder if I'll ever live in the city again.

"Marie," I say after milking, "do you know we're leaving tomorrow?"

"No!" she says, reaching out with a long, warm hug.

"Here are my cards," I say. I hand her my vocabulary cards, French on one side, English on the other. We hug and kiss again. "I'll miss you!"

I awake in the middle of the night, reflecting on our travel plans. Camilla will drive us to Beziers, and from there, we'll hitchhike south, from Spain to Morocco. My feelings toward Randy have fluctuated so much, but now I'm excited to share this new adventure.

On my last morning, I milk the goats, feed bottles to the babies who are separated from their moms, and give a special hug to Lucy. I pet Elusive, who will not permit a hug, rub the chin of Natasha, and stroke Frippo for the last time. How sad to leave my adopted family, the enchanting hills, and my little goats. The beauty of the mountains, the skies, and the aromatic thyme are as fresh and vibrant as the day I first arrived.

With the sun partially shrouded in fog, Randy and I scramble into the now-so-familiar tin car. As Camilla drives from the house to the road, the clomping of hooves sounds behind us. I stick my head out the window, the breeze on my face, and here comes Jacques, riding one of his wild Camargues, waving with his leather reins, "*À toute à l'heure!*"

Riding behind, Louis bounces on Mistral, barely keeping up. "*À toute à l'heure, Ay liz a bet a!*" he shouts.

Michel gallops along Randy's side of the car, followed by Jean on his horse, his smile as wide as the Pyrenee Mountains. Trotting along, keeping pace with the car, they escort us on horseback through the valley, all the way to the next village. With dampened eyes and a broad smile, I mouth, "*À toute à l'heure. À toute à l'heure !*"

Afterword

Our hitchhiking adventure was not entirely successful. After spending three days on the road from Beziers to Barcelona, a distance of 150 miles, Randy and I bought train tickets to Madrid. From there, we ventured to Fez, Morocco, back to Paris, and to several more European countries. We laughed in the countryside and fought in the cities. And, yes, we remained platonic. He traveled home to Australia in May, and I returned to America in June. We wrote every few weeks for a year.

One day I received a letter in unfamiliar handwriting from Australia. It was Randy's Dad, reporting that a brick flew off a lorry on the freeway and knocked Randy in the head. He slipped into a coma, and a month later, died.

I read the letter twice before I dropped it, shocked over news too impossible to believe. Randy and I had lived in a cocoon, like two people on a deserted island. My friend, my companion, my other half, now dead. I still mourn my precious, gentle friend.

I visited the farm in 1985 and again in 1999, unprepared for the changes. Camilla and Jacques divorced, with Jacques remaining on the farm and Camilla moving to the coast. Jacques remarried, and with his new wife, upgraded the farm. Inside, electricity flowed, along with a fax machine and modern plumbing. Why? Because instead of raising goats, Jacques had converted the property. We found a unique get-a-way for tourists, a rustic escape with a sweat lodge for New Age appeal. Though no goats, sheep, or an ornery pregnant cow, the Camargues horses still roamed the hills, as regal and stately as ever.

Michel owned a farm nearby and joined us for lunch. I heard that Marie lived in Paris; while Louis gained fame riding in a horse circus.

I visited Garner in Alaska. I originally bought a one-way ticket to Anchorage, but Susannah, my dear, wise friend Susannah, convinced me to exchange it for a round-trip.

The beauty of Alaska stunned me. "Yeah," Garner said with his understated wit, "Scenic overkill." We loved, he drank, and I said, no, really, no. I cannot live like this. I flew home two weeks after I arrived. Finally, we moved on, and lost touch with each other.

When I began to write this book, thirty years later, I searched for him on Facebook. I found a memorial page dedicated to Garner, created by his high school friends. I wrote to them and from them, gathered that Garner died alone, a heroin addict with hepatitis C on the streets of Seattle. Apparently, the coroner couldn't identify him at first. He came within minutes of being buried in a pauper's grave. Evidently, they tracked down his sister and that is how his friends learned of his death.

Susannah finished school at the community college, had another son, and moved to Seattle where she graduated from the university, the first person in her family to do so. She moved south to be closer to her parents and children and continues to work in social services. We see each other every year or so.

As for myself, I returned to America to a rare and delightful family reunion hosted by my sister on Cape Cod. From there, I gallivanted to Eugene for one more Oregon Country Faire. Then, the decision. Where to live?

After much thought, the rural peninsula near Seattle attracted me. In my first job I taught and befriended people with significant disabilities at a group home. This work suited me perfectly but, as so often happens in social services, I rose up the ladder. My life became administrative, so I returned to school to earn my Masters in Social Work.

And, then came Paul. When he and I first met, I told my roommate, "He's cute, but he does *data processing*. How boring!" Well, the love of my life turned out to be a computer genius, quite handy for an aspiring writer. We married, bore an incredible daughter, brilliant and beautiful, and I became a stay-at-home mom. Eventually, I returned to the University of Washington to follow my first passion, writing.

My home has never again been in the city. Being close to Nature remains essential to me, whether in the openness of the country or the water surrounding my island. I shrink in the city—contract, become hardened, irritate easily, become anxious. My life is fairly healthy now, with no drugs or sugar or alcohol. Exercise, meditation, and laughter play important roles in my life. I wasn't exactly yearning for a path to peace of mind when I backpacked to France, yet somehow, that's what I discovered on that mountainside west of the Mediterranean, north of the white jagged Pyrenees.

We hope you enjoyed A Long Way from Paris. *If you have questions or comments for the author, please contact her at truwryter@comcast.net, through her Web site at www.ecmurray.com, or on Twitter @UrbanGoatherd. Thank you!*

Acknowledgements

Thank you to the scores of people who helped me during the six years I spent writing this book. I once believed that being an author was a solitary venture. Not true! While I spent many hours, days, weeks writing alone, it is only with the support, insight, and words of encouragement that I finished this book.

Thank you to my editor and publisher, Jan Walker; for her seemingly endless patience teaching me, correcting errors, and answering countless questions. Thanks to my mentor, Theo Nestor, who set me on the right track. Both Meghan Stevenson and Rachel Moorhead not only offered tremendous insight, but knew more about goats and farming than I ever will. Anjali Banerjee's keen ability to dissect my work helped me clarify a number of issues in my manuscript. And thanks to Carol Wissmann who shaped the final manuscript with subtle, utterly helpful, tips.

I cannot say enough about my writers group whose words of wisdom and support propelled me forward during the six years I spent writing this book: Arissa Rench, Julie Gardner, Kristine Forbes, Steph Terrien, Laura Duncan

Boss, Barbara Boster, and Amanda Kelly. Wendy Hinman has held my hand as I stumbled down the final stretch.

Thanks to my friends, teachers, and readers: Roberta Brown Root, Ingrid Ricks, Langdon Cook, Jana Bourne, Carol Wissmann, Scott Driscoll, Maria Semple, Julia Glass, Robert Ginet, and Ryan Boudinot. I also thank my incredible family and friends for their support and encouragement: Susan Corcoran, Joan Steiger, Brenda Olson, Sari Clark, and the Murray-Nau-Squires clan. Thank you to Liam Salter, the Regnier family, and the Fenns. I am also incredibly grateful to my remarkable Teasters group. Thanks to all my fellow students in Theo's classes who sang *The Lonely Goatherd* when I first started on this project. Most of all, I am so grateful to Paul and Kristen Murray, for their love, devotion, and inspiration, and even those *boring* computer skills. Thank you!

CPSIA information can be obtained at www.ICGtesting.com
Printed in the USA
BVOW02s1419070815

411953BV00002B/34/P